Gender and God

GENDER & GOD

Love and Desire in Christian Spirituality

Rachel Hosmer

Printed in the United States of America by Cowley Publications.

International Standard Book No.: 0-936384-39-5

Cover design by Charles C. Hefling, Jr.

Library of Congress Cataloging-in-Publication Data

Hosmer, Rachel.
    Gender and God.

    1. Image of God. 2. Creation. 3. Spirituality.
I. Title.
BT701.2.H67 1986   233'.5   86-8980
ISBN 0-936384-39-5

parentibus meis

radicibus meis

in memoriam

Acknowledgments

I wish to thank those who have read and criticized the manuscript of this book, whose encouragement kept me at the long task of writing. First of all, my thanks are due to the sisters of the Manhattan house of our Order, without whose support I could never have brought the book to completion: Alicia Cristina Rivera, Jean Campbell, Cornelia Ransom, Rosina Ampah, Cintra Pemberton. Then I would like to thank my readers, Sister Frances Cole and Sister Kathryn Whittle; my friends from the General Theological Seminary, John and Elizabeth Koenig, and Patricia and Ronald Wilson-Kastner; Barbara Hall of Virginia Theological Seminary; and Janet Schulte, Sophia Wentz, and Diantha Hall.

A special debt is owed to Fontaine Maury Belford, who served as editorial consultant and helped me unlock the problems of revision, and Alvord Beardslee, who put his store of wisdom and knowledge at my disposal. To a succession of faculty secretaries at General Seminary my thanks are due for typing and retyping the manuscript: Sandra Ley, Gretchen Zimmerman, Lyn Larsen. To my editor, finally, Cynthia Shattuck, I owe thanks for the wisdom and patience which guided me through and helped me bring the enterprise to completion.

Rachel Hosmer, OSH

CONTENTS

Introduction

The questions which drew this book out of me came
from my own experience, as all deep questions do, so I shall
begin with a personal statement. I am a woman, a nun, a
teacher, a priest, and a spiritual director. The Christian
tradition which has informed my life is that of the Episcopal
Church, my mother's church and my own since my teens. I
have also received a great deal from other Christian traditions
— Roman Catholic, Orthodox, Protestant — as well as from
non-Christian traditions such as Judaism and the East.
Similarly I have learned much from the intellectual probing
of New England dissent and even from unbelief. At the
same time I am convinced that some of the doctrines my
forebears rejected were indeed worthy of rejection.
Whatever threads of consistency keep this book together,
however, derive from a Christian world view, and I hold that
view by faith. It is not, I hope, a blind faith, unwilling or
afraid to listen to other voices or to reconsider positions in
the light of new questions and insights. Nevertheless my
experience is one of returning time and time again, after
bouts of questioning and debating, to a reaffirmation of my
baptismal commitment on a deeper level than before.
A catechism which I learned as a child from the
American Prayer Book of 1892 linked our baptismal
commitment to a simple question of identity: "What is your
name?" it asked. "Who gave you this name?" The reply
was, "My sponsors in baptism, wherein I was made a member
of Christ, the child of God and an inheritor of the kingdom
of heaven." I would quarrel now with the implication that I
was not "the child of God" before my baptism, but the old

[1]

words do give a concrete and objective answer to the
question of identity. This is who I am, member of Christ,
child of God, inheritor of the kingdom.

We live in a time which increasingly demands that we
reexamine what have been assumed to be the "givens" of our
tradition. Liberation theology asserts the necessary
identification of the church with those whose needs and very
being society has failed to affirm: the poor, Blacks, women,
the culturally, economically and psychologically oppressed.
Creation theology emphasizes the positive values of created
persons and things in contrast to salvation theology, which
emphasizes deliverance from evil by the act of God. The
struggle of women for ordination has just begun in some
traditions, and the emergence of a body of scholarship
dealing with the experience — historical, economic, social,
cultural, biological and psychological — of women, has
necessitated a reexamination of many biases. All of these
things make us aware of the need to examine some of the
theological themes which have shaped traditional Christian
spirituality.

My book began to take shape around the necessity I
perceived for this kind of exploration. Its basis is a series of
lectures I gave at Shrinemont, Virginia in 1982, for the
Diocesan Association of Christian Educators, on the theme
"Feminine/Masculine: Image of God." Since then I have
reworked and expanded the original material, but have kept
to the main outline of the lectures. My original audience was
a group of professional educators, mostly women, and I still
have them and their counterparts in my mind as I write now.
Both the lectures and the book, however, are addressed to all
women and men who are concerned with what the Christian
church teaches us about ourselves and about who we are,
female and male, and yet at the same time wish to preserve
the integrity of our tradition.

The theme I have chosen is our creation, male and
female, in the divine image. It is a theme that illuminates
our self-understanding and our relationship with God and

with each other. We shall consider this theme in the light of biblical teaching and the tradition of the church. We shall also consider it in the light of what our understanding of liberation theology and creation theology can tell us of the broader implications of the gift of life that resembles God's own — the inner dynamism of the triune God.

The form of the book is a combination of expository chapters with short prologues containing more personal commentary on the main chapters. It was only after I had written the first draft that I realised from the comments of my readers that I was speaking in two voices — one personal, arising from my imagination and memory, and one more objective and scholarly. The dissonance troubled me, but I could not decide which to eliminate. My solution was to retain both voices but to keep them distinct, and use the more personal style to comment on the expository material.

Three chief metaphors have guided me through the writing and helped me to organize the diverse material. Two others arose as I sought for more contemporary metaphors for the image of God in us. The first three images are the chariot, the net, and the keys. The chariot is drawn from Plato's dialogue, the *Phaedrus*, and suggests a spirituality of ascent, of mastery and the love of excellence. In various forms the ladder, the mountain, and degrees of love or of humility are all metaphors that dominate much traditional spirituality from the Greek Fathers to our own day. By contrast, the net is a more biblical metaphor, speaking of community and connectedness. Rather than the upward thrust of the chariot image, the net suggests a lateral pull, drawing things together. In Scripture the net often refers to a trap or snare, but in Matthew's gospel Jesus uses it in order to point to the Kingdom: "the kingdom of heaven is like a net which was thrown into the sea and gathered fish of every kind" (Mt. 13:47). Here I use it as a metaphor for comprehensiveness and relationship.

Keys are also a biblical metaphor. In the Hebrew scriptures, they are symbols of the power both to close, deny, and reject and to open and release: "And I will place on his shoulder the key of the house of David: he shall open and none shall shut, and he shall shut and none shall open" (Is. 22:22). In Matthew's gospel the keys stand for the power given to the apostles as representatives of the messianic community, to bind or to loose, to forgive sin or retain it (Mt. 16:19). For me, the keys speak of the opposing uses of power — locking up and unlocking, forbidding and liberating. It is an ambiguous image, one of both dominance and liberation.

Two contemporary metaphors I will use for the image of God in us are those of genetic imprint and of gravity. The first refers to the integral and ineffaceable patterning of the structure of the human being that marks each one of us as a fresh creation, unique and unrepeatable. I use it by extension in order to describe inner structures of relationships and collectives. Finally, the basic design of creation I call "gravity." The dynamism of gravity exerts a pull that keeps the parts of the universe in existence and in tension. It maintains them in relationship as one pull counteracts another. The great general law is that bodies, masses, attract one another. In the context of this book, gravity is a metaphor for the love that binds creation into a living, interacting, and corporate whole.

My procedure will be to begin with some biblical material which is closely related to the theme of the divine image in us. This is of real importance, particularly for women who today are coming to a new understanding of themselves in ways which differ radically from many of our inherited ideas about our nature and social function. Parents, teachers, pastors, and spiritual guides all need to readjust some of their attitudes toward gender differences and find ways to nourish children in new ways. Of crucial importance to all of us is the acceptance of men's and women's sexuality as given by God and as imaging God. We are most "like" God in mutuality, in our relationships, in friendship and marriage, and in our meeting and interacting on every level with the opposite — the other.

The biblical creation stories in Genesis, with their account of the making of the first woman from the rib of the first man, and the command of God to this first human couple to have dominion over the earth and its creatures, have been used to justify both the unrestrained use of the earth and its fruits and creatures, and the domination of women by men. These stories suggest that God shared the divine prerogative of domination with the first man and hence with men of succeeding generations. Clearly any consideration of the theology of the divine image in us must begin with the Bible.

From Christian tradition I have chosen to discuss some writers whom I love and whose works I have read and pondered over a good deal: Gregory of Nyssa, Augustine, Dante and Julian of Norwich. I have chosen Gregory because his writings provide a good example of the spirituality of ascent, and because he is one of the first theologians to deal in detail with the meaning of creation in the image of God. Augustine I have chosen because he was the first to teach that we are created in the image of the Trinity. Augustine, together with Thomas Aquinas, represents a negative attitude toward sexuality and toward women — the belief that woman is not, in herself, made in the image of God, but shares the image only through her subordination to the man. Even in these authors, however, there are surprising insights and positive images of the feminine in which we can rejoice and from which we can learn. Dante's vision of God is mediated through *eros*, love, and love centered and evoked by a particular concrete and historical woman, Beatrice. Julian has much to say about the motherhood of God, about Jesus as our Mother, and about the Holy Trinity as the pattern and image of the divine in us. Finally I shall look at a few contemporary writers and at my own experience, and try to see how we may receive and

understand in a different way what it means to be female
and male, masculine and feminine, in the image of God.

*"God created humankind in the divine image; in God's
own image God created us, female and male."*
In this book I shall attempt to explore the meaning of
this statement as it relates to our understanding of ourselves
and our spirituality. In the primal creative act of God, the
divine image is imprinted upon human beings of two genders.
One image is reflected by two beings, male and female, who
share a common humanity. It is in this connectedness with
each other, this capacity for relationship with the other, that
we human beings manifest the image of our creator.
There are many definitions of spirituality, and I suppose
all of them are tentative and incomplete. They point toward
something without ever reaching it. Christian spirituality can
be thought of as our personal experience of God through
Christ, in community and in solitude. It can also be thought
of as an objective field of study, with a history, having
connections with philosophy and theology, and with
implications for social institutions. Nothing is automatically
good about our spirituality except its source. The gift of
spiritual life entails both freedom and responsibility. We can
make a mess of our lives, or a glorious achievement, or
something in between. The moment the Spirit touches our
flesh, animating us, it yields itself to our use of it.
Eventually we can obscure the divine image; there are
perversions of the spirit as well as shining examples of
holiness. Our faith tells us, however, as does some dim inst-
inctive hope, that we can never entirely obliterate the divine
image in ourselves. We are irrevocably rooted in God
through the given Spirit. All of God's gifts are given for our
joy, and reveal God reflected in our experience as person, in
community, and in our participation in the whole created
order. The life they reflect is the divine life of the Trinity,
reflected not in separate lists of qualities — one for men and

one for women — but in relationship itself, in the going out from self to the other, and the receiving of the other into the self.

Above, my reversal of the usual biblical sequence from "male and female" to "female and male" is intended as a counterpoise of the biblical order, a complementary formula suggesting that neither gender is prior to or superior to the other. One can as well begin with the female as the male. The terms "female" and "male" refer to biological differences which are easily discernible. When it comes to psychological and emotional differences between the sexes, however, and the use of words "feminine" and "masculine" to connote qualities, aptitudes, proclivities, weaknesses, and strengths, the semantic situation is far from clear. Our ideas about "feminine" and "masculine" are richer in their connotations, but less clearly defined, than those about "female" and "male." The words feminine and masculine refer not to biological sex, but to spiritual, psychological, and emotional qualities associated with each gender. These associations, however, are vague and debatable and tend to differ with different ages and places.

Many cultures as well as our own are dominated by gender stereotypes. A "good man" is strong and brave, objective and clear in his thinking, consistent and resolute, while a "good woman" is gentle, patient, submissive and cooperative. One way of avoiding stereotyping is to remember that whatever we may attribute to one always has its counterpart in the other. Women can be clearheaded and men can be gentle. Just as each gender has physical analogues of the opposite gender, so with the qualities. What we call feminine qualities, for instance, can predominate in a male, and vice versa — and not necessarily as distortions.

Some of the stereotyping derives from external physical differences between male and female, but cultural influences seem to produce most of it. In a primitive hunting culture, for example, tasks were divided between the sexes out of necessity. The men went out to hunt and the women stayed

at home with the stores and the babies, a very practical
division of labor, as well as a necessary one, since babies had
to be breast-fed. Staying at home and caring for the stores
and the babies requires one set of aptitudes; going out to
hunt requires another. In agricultural societies some tasks
also became the province of one gender and others the
province of the opposite, but the assignment of these roles
was not consistent. In some societies planting was done by
men and weeding and harvesting by women, weaving by men
and pottery by women, while other cultures reversed these
assignments. Technological and cultural changes in our own
day have also required corresponding changes in the ideals
assigned to each of the genders.

In the Bible we have examples of women that begin to
move away from the stereotype and instead show a rich
diversity. In the thirty-first chapter of Proverbs we have the
portrait of a woman as a shrewd and robust manager of a
large and prosperous household. She is busy, hard-working,
vigorous, and productive; she is canny in business and kind
to the poor, a strength and support to her husband and
household, for "she opens her mouth with wisdom, and the
teaching of kindness is on her tongue" (31:26). In the Old
Testament there are aggressive and war-like women such as
Jael, credited with killing an enemy general (Judges 4), and
prophetesses like Deborah from the days of the Judges in
Israel, and like Huldah, who validated for King Josiah the
authenticity of the Book of the Law discovered in the
Temple (II Kings: 22:3-20). In the New Testament Anna the
prophetess was in the Temple when Mary and Joseph brought
Jesus to the priest to present him to the Lord (Lk. 2:36-8).
There are queens like Jezebel who exhibit leadership,
judgment, and aggressiveness — similarly there are men who
show delicacy and compassion — David in his dealings with
Saul and in his friendship with Jonathan, and Jesus in his
dealings with sinners, outcasts, women and children.

There are many theories about gender differences today,
and much research goes on with debatable conclusions. Our

experience as women and as men seems to point to possibilities of development for both women and men undreamed of in earlier ages. One result, clearly, is that "masculine" and "feminine" are terms not always restricted to male and female, respectively, but which can be interchangeable. Nevertheless, stereotyping has a long history and still has influence not only on how we label qualities, but also on how we value them.

This has a special bearing upon our understanding of the divine image in us as members of the great collectivities of our day: political, economic, and industrial systems. More and more writers are calling our attention to the dangers which the human race and the planet which is our home now face. We know that an increasing population and an expanding economy threaten to exhaust the resources of food and energy upon which we all depend. We are aware of increasing pollution, acid rain, toxic dumps, the extinction of species and the destruction of ecosystems. We have begun to master the earth, and she is in danger of death from our misuse of her fertility. Is there some relationship between the attitude of the "developed" countries to world resources and to "underdeveloped" cultures and peoples, and the value we place on intellect and power? Have we as a race regarded ourselves as lords of creation rather than as her servants and friends? Can we find in the Bible and in our Christian tradition teaching which encourages respect for the nurturing and serving qualities that are of crucial importance to our survival? Human collectivities — churches, nations, corporations — are made up of human individuals. Each of us is especially called today to help right the balance between masculine and feminine values. We need to reassert the worth of mutuality, self-sacrificing love, humility and vulnerability.

Image and Likeness

Before addressing myself to the interpretation of the text in Genesis 1:27, which concerns our creation, male and female, in the image of God, I need to say something about how I understand the faith in the Church that the Bible is the word of God, and something about the method of Bible study I have been taught and which I try to use as faithfully as I can.

My earliest encounters with the Bible were both negative and positive. My father, who, I must say, was at best a luke-warm member of the Unitarian Church to which he seldom went, liked to read aloud to us children from the words of Tom Paine and William Lecky and other critics of Christianity. He often held forth on the follies of the fundamentalists. Before I ever read Genesis for myself, I was convinced that it was a superstitious and unscientific account of the beginning of things, filled with contradictions and absurdities. I had no reason to expect much of the rest of the Bible either, and I adopted a skeptical attitude toward the idea of biblical inspiration and revelation.

A more positive attitude, however, tempered the negative one. It was communicated to me indirectly, partly by my mother, who taught us to pray the Our Father and "heard our prayers" at night, and partly by the simple devotion of some of the people who worked for us. One of the most influential was a black woman named Mary Noble, whom my mother taught to read and write. She knew, believed and loved the Bible, its stories and its teaching, and she loved and cared for me and my brothers when we were children. She sheltered us when she could from the consequences of our naughtiness, separated us when he fought, and yet did not

[10]

spoil us. I remember how she dressed down my older brother when he put our youngest brother, naked, in among the hens in the yard for a joke. She rushed in, seized the little boy, and covered him with her apron, crying, "What are you doing to *my child*?" She carried him into the house, comforted him and restored him to his clothing.

I had a secret feeling that Mary Noble's ideas about God and the Bible were right, and that my father's were wrong.

Neither parent invoked divine sanctions for household discipline, and I was not exposed to the notion that a watchful and vengeful deity was keeping tabs on me and would one day catch up with me. Common sense, accepted standards of decent and reasonably considerate behavior toward others, and my parents' own convictions about right and wrong were behind their dealings with our willfulness and waywardness. Believing something depended on whether it made sense to oneself and others. When later in life I learned about the Anglican attitude to authority, which requires one to balance the text of Scripture, its interpretation in tradition, and one's own experience and sense of the truth, it was an attitude very congenial to me. Yet perhaps most important of all in determining my attitude to the Bible was my early impression that Mary Noble had a "window into glory" that I did not have, and which bore some relationship to the Bible and to my experience of her as a wise, warm, and loving person.

Not until I entered religious life in 1928 was I exposed to anything like regular Bible reading. Novitiates in those days were not places where scholarly pursuits were much encouraged. The historical and critical approach to Bible study, moreover, which had caused as much uproar in the church as Darwin's theories had done, was generally regarded with suspicion in convents. Our Bible study was uncomplicated by critical theory. When I began teaching Christian Doctrine in secondary school a few years later, I did encounter some of the basic positions of the biblical scholars of that day, but it was not until 1966, when I returned to school myself at Union Theological Seminary in New York, that I made a sustained effort to master the contemporary techniques of biblical interpretation.

The result for me was a surge of fresh interest in the Bible, and a deep delight in pondering the words of Scripture, which has never left me. It was enlightening to get back to the original language, to learn more about the historical and cultural background of the Bible, and to begin to distinguish in a more systematic way the periods and circumstances from which particular passages emerged, as well as the literary forms used in that ancient literature. It was helpful, for instance, to begin to see the differences between material from early nomadic times and later writings from the time of the kings, as well as between prophecy before and during the Exile. In the New Testament also, it was equally helpful to recognize the differences between the early and later work of Paul, and between his genuine work and the later writings attributed to him.

It was impressed upon us at Union that we had never completed our interpretation of a Bible passage until we had taken the responsibility not only for conveying what it meant for the writer at the time and for the original audience, but also what it means now for us and for our time.

I have no claim to being a biblical scholar. My interpretation of Scripture does begin with my own effort to use the tools at my command for penetrating to the original meaning of a text, but I also depend heavily upon the conclusions of others. In the end, of course, it is my responsibility to find a way through conflicting interpretations, and to avoid reading into the words of Scripture what I want them to say. My father was partly right — there *are* contradictions in the Bible, outworn laws and customs, and bits of folk wisdom of limited scope and limited value for our day. There are also puzzles and dead places which I must leave aside until illumination comes. But Mary Noble was right, too. She taught me by her life that the Bible *is* the word of God, and that its over-arching meaning is the compassionate, dependable love of God. All those centuries God worked through the rough-hewn Hebrew language and grammar, the tales and customs of the ancient Near East and the bloody history of those years, to get God's own message through to us all in Scripture.

Today it is often the metaphors in the Bible that seem to speak to me most powerfully. The scriptural images do more than delight and intrigue, even more than challenge and judge — they actually communicate the truth and energy of the divine wisdom.

I think of the word of God as seed, or as bread, or as fire, or as a two-edged sword, active and alive, strong to purify, energize, and transform.

The method of Bible study that I have been taught and which I have used in this book is the one generally described as "critical," as distinct from "fundamentalist" or "literalist." "Critical" comes from a Greek root that means "distinguish." A critical method of interpretation, when applied to the Bible, is one which distinguishes between the literal and spiritual meaning, between different literary forms and sources, and between various levels of editorial work. The distinction between the literal or historical meaning of a work, and its spiritual meaning, is a very ancient one. It was used in classical times to interpret Homer, for instance, and in the time of Jesus and of Paul it was used by a scholarly Jew, Philo, to interpret the Hebrew scriptures. Modern methods are more sophisticated forms of the same basic approach and their acceptance is part of the inheritance of Christian scholarship today. Some Anglicans were among the first to accept this method of interpreting Scripture when it was proposed by 19th century biblical scholars in Germany.

When we read and try to understand the meaning of biblical texts for our own day, we must realize that we are confronting a collection of books written originally in Hebrew and Greek over a span of a thousand years and formed by the culture of the ancient Near East. Because we believe that the Bible contains the word of God, we try to distinguish between what the texts meant for the audiences for whom they were originally written and their meaning for us today. Some things to be borne in mind as we do this concern first the texts themselves, and then the way they have been understood in different ages and situations.

When we focus upon the meaning of the texts of the Hebrew scriptures as they were originally written, we make distinctions between different literary forms. Legendary material, stories, riddles, parables, songs and proverbs differ from chronicles and law codes, and differ again from sermons, prayers and prophetic utterances. "History" as we think of it today did not exist in ancient times. This recognition of different literary forms helps us find the meaning of the text. Legends and stories are not used to establish historicity, songs are not the basis of laws, and chronicles do not give us prophetic insight.

As to the texts themselves, several things need to be pointed out. In all cultures, songs and stories are preserved and transmitted orally before they are written down. The editorial processes involved in the transition are human ones and subject to error and to bias. Everything in the Bible, of course, was written down by hand. Copyists, like typists and computer operators, make mistakes. When material from different sources was put together to form a larger whole, ancient writers felt no need to identify their sources. It was a literary convention, in classical times, to attribute authorship not always to the actual writer, but to some well-known person whom one wished to honor and whose name would give weight to the work in question. For example, the book we know as Isaiah was actually written in three parts, at different times and by different people. The name Isaiah of Jerusalem, whose ministry forms the core of chapters 1-39, was given to the whole. Chapters 40-55 are by a later hand, now referred to as Second Isaiah, and the final chapters a collection of even later oracles.

A distinction can also be made between the work of one editor and another. The material of Scripture existed first in oral form and then was recorded at different times and places by different people with distinct interests and styles, and finally worked into something resembling its present form by an editor or series of editors.

Recognizing the ways that the words of Scripture have been preserved and handed down helps us understand at least to some extent what the text meant as it was originally written. Rather than *originals*, what we have are copies of copies made centuries later, and passed from hand to hand. We have also to remember that we are dealing with translations, from Hebrew to Greek to Latin, and much later to the vernacular.

In what follows we will try to see as clearly as we can what the original text of the creation stories in Genesis meant to its first hearers, and then discern what we can of what it says to us now. We have to bear in mind that the most difficult and risky distinction is the one each of us must make in discerning what God is saying for our own time, through the words and images of an ancient culture. We shall consider the contrast between the two creation stories themselves as well as the further contrast between what they say and what they have been thought to say. Only then can we begin to discern what they say to us now.

Much of the Old Testament is poetry, I have been told by my teachers. "Poetry is like a finger pointing to the moon," says a Zen master.[1] Poetry, like theology, serves to point us toward a place at which we can never arrive because it is beyond us, beyond our consciousness, our limitedness. It draws us toward something larger, more universal, deeper. The creation stories, being both poetry and theology, should be read as metaphor. They point, without ever reaching, toward the mystery of God as creator.

Every culture has its stock of stories about beginnings and endings. These stories answer the questions we all ask at

some time in our life about origins and final destinies, our
own and those of the other creatures and people around us.
Why has the blue jay got bars on his wings? Where do cats
come from? Who makes the snow? Who made me? Where
is grandmother now? Such stories, on the nature of things,
are not histories. We were not there in the beginning, and
the final end of creation has not yet come, so we do not
know what that will be like. The stories that deal with these
questions are called creation myths. Their imaginative terms
capture and preserve the insight and wisdom of ancient
ancestors who struggled with the questions before us. The
Bible stories about creation are of this genre. They differ
markedly, however, from other creation stories in other
cultures in several respects.

Folk stories and creation myths the world over, like
fingers pointing to the moon, attempt to show us something
of our ultimate meaning. When we ask what the Bible
teaches us about sex we think, many of us, of Eve and the
apple. Let's look at this story and the related material in the
first chapter of Genesis — which means birth, or beginning.
"In the beginning, God..." we read. We all know the story,
and we think we know its meaning: it is a story about Adam
and Eve, the first man and the first woman. Eve tempted
Adam to commit the primal sin, the sin of disobedience to
God. Henceforth she is put by God under the domination of
her husband. This is her punishment and it continues to this
day. The story as some have come to interpret it is the basis
of a widespread cultural assumption about sexuality: men are
superior to women as the result of the sin of a woman, a sin
for which all women bear the responsibility. It is, therefore,
the will of God that the sexes should be related to each other
primarily through the domination of the female by the male.

When we look at the biblical texts more closely, we see
that there are two creation stories in Genesis. The first is the
so-called Priestly account, or P story (Gen. 1:1-2:4a), while
the second is the Yahwist, or J, story (Gen. 2:4b-3:24). The J
account comes after P in the text as we have it, but in fact

[16]

was put together centuries before. In between the writing down of these two accounts of human origins came the major catastrophe in the history of the people of God: the destruction of the Temple and the holy city of Jerusalem, exile in Babylon, and the extinction of the royal line of David. So the Priestly account of creation was written in priestly circles during the Exile by writers who looked back through the history of their people and conserved and reinterpreted ancient material. The P story is an abstract, highly-polished theological account and it contains our key verse, "So God created man in his own image; in the image of God he created him; male and female he created them" (1:27). It begins with a theological statement of central import: "In the beginning, God." In contrast with other creation stories, which begin with some *thing* — a turtle, an egg, a stony hillside, a snake, the tongue of a shoe — the biblical story is about imposing order upon a formless chaos, from which the creator made sun and moon and earth and all living things. The Hebrew verb for "create" is only used in the Bible with God as its subject, and never with a word denoting the material from which a thing is made. It connotes creation out of chaos. The God who made all things from chaos is neither a warrior nor a begetter; God is a creator.

In creating human beings God made a human pair, male and female, in the divine image. The word for human being is *adam*, from *adamah*, earth. It can be translated "earth-creature": no sexual difference is indicated. The original human was not androgynous, but a unity. Sexual distinction is a quality imparted to an already existing being who is in the image of God. The story is a metaphor, a finger pointing to the moon. It is meant to explain the origin of something known in experience, that is, sexual difference, as well as to answer the more general question of the origin of humankind. We may note here that in the P story, feminine and masculine are created simultaneously. There is no suggestion of superiority or inferiority even though the masculine word comes first in the text.

The first human creatures together are in the image of their creator and to them, as a representative of their maker, the Lord of all, is given the responsibility of looking after the rest of creation. *Ha-adam* is male and female, and is referred to as "them." Relation is implied only in the connective *and*. Male and female are involved with each other; together they are *ha-adam*. The tasks assigned them, to dominate the rest of creation and to be responsible for procreation, are assigned to both together. So far the Genesis story offers no basis for sexual stereotypes. "The image of God" is a phrase that points toward something unknown, toward the hidden God. Sexual difference does not describe God. He is not masculine or feminine, nor a combination, nor an androgyne.

In the second and third chapters of Genesis (2:4b-3:24) the J story offers us a very different creation myth. This story deals not only with the origin of human beings, but also with the origin of suffering, toil, and death, and with the powerful drive of sexuality. If the P story is doctrine, the J story is narrative, concerned with the effects of the disintegration of an original harmony. The style of the writing — clear, objective, simple, and concrete — is better suited to story-telling than to theology. God appears in human form and shows concern about the human being in the garden. The style, which is "glass-like, transparent, fragile," makes exposition difficult but the meaning is plain.[2] The J account wrestles with the problems of the origin of sin, pain, toil and death, as well as of human origins, whereas the P story focuses upon the single issue of the creation of humankind.

The J narrative has an introduction and three movements. In the introduction (2:4b-7) heaven and earth are created and the earth-creature, *ha-adam*, is made out of earth and water, clay, molded by the creator and inspired by him with the breath of life. The creature of clay becomes a living being.

God bends over to breathe into the earth-creature God's own breath, which is life.

Ha-adam enters into a garden, a place of delight, and receives the gift of life and the blessing of God. The likeness between God and the earth-creature is apparent, and so is the loving dependence of the creature upon the brooding love of the creator.

In the first movement, Genesis 2:8-25, love emerges in human experience. The setting is the lovely garden, a park of trees, paradise. In the middle are two trees: the tree of life and the tree of the knowledge of good and evil. It is a garden for pleasure, for joy, and it needs careful tending. The garden is located in time and space. The Lord God put *ha-adam* in the garden to till and to take care of it, to be its servant. God gives responsibility to the earth-creature to nurture, not to plunder and rape, the garden of trees.

A prohibition is given. There are limits set to the human dominion over creation. God says that some food is not good for *ha-adam*, who is forbidden to eat from the tree of the knowledge of good and evil. To eat the fruits of the other trees is allowed, but to eat the fruit of this tree is forbidden. Limits are set for God's vice-regent, representative, and steward. The purpose of the command is to give order, nourishment, and growth to human life. The tree of life, the tree of the knowledge of good and evil, means everything in human experience. To understand good and evil is to be omniscient. The Hebrew verb "to know" does not mean pure intellection, but includes experience and communion. So the tree of the knowledge of good and evil is also a tree of experience.[3]

At this point God reflects upon the newly-created living being and says, "It is not good for *ha-adam* to be alone." So animals are created, and birds, and brought to *ha-adam* in order to be named, but they are not made in the image of God and cannot satisfy the human longing for companionship and the human need for collaboration. Solitude here is loneliness and helplessness. The earth-creature needs help both in its inner life and its outward task of tending the garden. At this point God puts *ha-adam* into a deep sleep, as for an operation. The new creation goes unobserved. The divine act alters the very nature of *ha-adam*. Two new words emerge in the Hebrew text: for the first time we have *ish*, man, and *ishah*, woman. Now God's earth-creature experiences mutual relationship. Together man and woman become one flesh, and in The Song of Songs, a later commentary on the creation story, the bond between them of conjugal love is "stronger than death" (8:6).

God is now imaged in human relationship, in complementarity, mutuality, and in the risky, trusting act of self-giving: the leaving of self and the going out from self to enter the unknown life of the other. On the historical level the story is about development, the unfolding of life. It points toward the meaning of human life as fulfillment of joy in the harmony of opposites, whence love emerges, the image of God.

The first movement of the J story, then, is about this emergence of love and the meaning and limit of obedience. The second movement, Genesis 2:25—3:6, is about disobedience and the breakup of harmony and love. It is not about sexual sin. The man and the woman — as they are now called — confront the paradox of their situation. They are dependent upon God, their creator, and they are responsible for the earth and its other creatures as well as for each other. This movement of the J story forces us to confront the paradox which we glimpse in every temptation, ranging from our minute scrupulosities to the temptations to selfishness, greed, envy, and pride that arise in our daily congress with others. We have to confront the stark and awful possibility of refusing the divine gifts of healing and forgiveness, choosing instead a final separation from the life of God. Our choices are real and our security against loneliness and death, like that of the first human beings in the story, is in obedience to God.

The actual disobedience occurs through an intermediary, the serpent. There is a play on words here. The man and woman are together, naked, *arummim*, and enter the crafty one, the *arum*. The serpent here is the interlocutor and the catalyst of the story, not the devil or an evil spirit, but the one whose function it is to test and to tempt the human pair. In the dialogue which ensues, the woman speaks for both the man and herself. To the serpent's clever and apparently innocent opening question, "Did God say, 'You shall not eat of any tree in the garden'?" she makes a comprehensive reply: "God said, 'You shall not eat of the fruit of the tree which is in the midst of the garden, neither shall you touch it, lest you die.'" The woman explains, distinguishes and applies to behavior the words of God. She is the respondent, the one responsible for the choice of obedience over against disobedience of the female/male. The serpent replies, challenges her, refutes her, lays claim himself to absolute knowledge: "You will not die." She believes him and eats. The serpent effectively destroys the harmony and well-being of the human couple to whom God has given authority over him.

God is silent.

The woman's disobedience is active. She finds the fruit pleasing, takes it, eats it and gives it to the man who is with her. The man is passive and silent, not reluctant: "And he ate."

The third movement in the story is about the disintegration of love. Genesis 3:8-24 describes the results of disobedience to God as an explanation of the human experience of suffering and death.

Death is the final destiny of the human pair. Enmity with the earth is symbolized both by the change in relationship between the serpent and the human pair — "They shall strike your head and you shall strike at their heel" — and by the cursing of the earth, which is now to bear thorns and thistles and require hard toil if it is to bring forth something edible. As for the man and the woman, they are now no longer equal partners, sharing the blessings and responsibilities of the garden, but subject to lust; the man is now master of the woman. God drives them both out of the place of delight, the garden of their felicity, and pronounces sentence upon them "Dust you are, and to dust you shall return" (Gen. 3:19b).

In place of collaboration and companionship, strife appears at every level. The disobedience which separates the human pair from God is mirrored through all the orders of creation. When the man and the woman cease to reflect the bond of the image, the ordering of love toward the other which reflects the inner life of God, the divine ordering of all creation suffers as well. The *ish* blames the *ishah* who blames the serpent. Imperfections become problems instead of promises, and guilt and remorse appear. Distinctions, which before denoted variety and richness and created the possibility of interplay, become burdened with labels of "inferiority" and "superiority." The supremely important distinction between the sexes, which makes possible new life and so much joy and growth and movement, becomes heavy with reproaches. It was the woman's fault. She is not only punished for her fault — she is laden with the burden of the world's guilt, all down the ages. A terrible new perspective opens for the human race as order becomes oppression and violence, and murder and warfare appear in history. The picture darkens as whole social attitudes and customs more and more reflect the brokenness of the bond of love which was meant to unite all of creation.

In the J story of the Fall, the man blames the woman and justifies himself: "She tempted me and I ate." Joy becomes tragedy and life ends in a return to the original clay in death. *Ha-adam* becomes male and female, and they are expelled from Eden into the stream of time and history.

Our understanding of the story must now be modified. The narrative is not about Adam and Eve, but about the first human being and the subsequent creation of the first human couple. *Ha-adam* is made in God's image; Adam and Eve

[22]

are names given to masculine and feminine *after* the disobedience. Notions of male superiority and female inferiority arise only after the disobedience, a consequence of it, not part of the original pattern of creation. Woman takes the lead in conversing with the serpent; together man and woman succumb to the tempting of the crafty one. Neither is cursed; both are punished.

The Old Testament almost never refers again to these stories; it does not interpret, expand, or comment further. After this Eve disappears, while the theme of the image and likeness does not recur. In a few places the imagery is there, but not the central meaning of the Fall story which points to the meaning, the naming, of what took place as a divine judgment. We shall see that the New Testament has more to say on the stories of creation and fall.

What does develop is Israel's growing perception that God is not only powerful and righteous, ruler and judge, but also tender and compassionate, loving spontaneously and warmly, merciful to the just and the unjust. God not only cares for the poor and oppressed, but sees in them the faithful remnant and confirms to them the divine promises.[4] It is through the righteous remnant, the poor and dispossessed of the land, that salvation will come.

Through the fall of Jerusalem, the destruction of the city and the Temple there emerged in Israel a new and poignant recognition of the relationship between suffering, judgment, humility, and forgiveness. The people of God learned through their deepest and most devastating defeat not that God had somehow lost a battle, but that another aspect of God's life had been uncovered from deep underneath the bloody rubble. Israel learned to recognize the righteousness and glory of God not in acts of conquest, but in divine mercy upon the poor and humble, in the motherly love of the Father. In her image of God the dimension of tenderness and patient care emerged alongside the dominating and masterful divine qualities. It is not, however, a question of either/or, but of both/and. Metaphors of maternal mercy and paternal concern for justice together point toward the one God. Developments in the New Testament and in later Christian tradition will show something of how succeeding generations interpreted the Psalmist's metaphor of meeting: "Steadfast love and faithfulness will meet;/righteousness and peace will kiss each other./Faithfulness will spring up from the ground,/and righteousness will look down from the sky" (Ps. 85:10–11).

A New Creation

Critical interpretation of the New Testament requires the same care in distinguishing sources, literary forms, and editorial additions and corrections as are required in reading the Hebrew scriptures. There are also many aspects of New Testament study which are peculiar to this literature. When the four gospels are compared, it is evident that three of the synoptics depend upon a basic sequence of events, and have some close interconnections and verbal similarities, while the fourth gospel has a different organizing scheme. More basic to our understanding of the texts is the fact that while we have whole letters of Paul and other writers, the chief character, Jesus of Nazareth, left no writings at all. What we know of him comes to us through the recorded recollections of others, some of whom may have known him in the flesh, but most of whom, including the Apostle Paul, encountered him only after the resurrection and learned of his life and teaching from earlier witnesses. These records come down to us in the four New Testament gospels. The first three, Matthew, Mark and Luke, are called the synoptics, because they employ a common time frame. The fourth gospe', attributed to John, uses a different chronology and literary structure and comes from a different milieu.

Each of the synoptics is not only intricately related to each other, but also possesses its own singularity of style and its own special interest and point of view. The current theological climate, the special needs of early Christian congregations, the social and political circumstances, as well as the personal preferences, insights, prejudices and emphases of each writer all influence the formulation of the texts. In

dealing with the gospels, scholars have attempted to
distinguish between the original words of Jesus, the selection
and application of these words made by the original hearers
who remembered and reported them, and the editor who
collected, arranged and recorded them.

While I accept all this and its importance, and endeavor
in the best way I can to apply it in my work, I also believe
that we can discern one historical flesh-and-blood Jesus when
we look along the trajectory of any one gospel. The gospels
converge upon one person. Their differences are subjective,
important because the subjective is true, and is the only
evidence we have. But the reality of the one human life of
Jesus is a reality which transcends the differences. It seems
to be true to say, "It is the Lord." However myopic or
astigmatic the lenses, I am sure I am looking through the
verbal levels of the New Testament toward the Lord, the
Christ, Jesus the promised Messiah, sent from the one the
Hebrews knew as Lord and Father and Creator, whom today
we are beginning to know also as Mother and Nurturer and
Pain-bearer for us all.

When we come to the writings of Paul, the problems are
somewhat different. We begin by sorting out the authentic
letters from the letters attributed to him, but coming from a
later time and from different circumstances. For example,
the Epistle to the Hebrews was at one time attributed to Paul,
but almost no New Testament scholar today would accept this
attribution. It has also been established that some of the
other New Testament epistles also attributed to Paul, notably
I and II Timothy and Titus, cannot have been written in their
present form by him. The Pauline authorship of II
Thessalonians, Ephesians and Colossians is disputed. Further,
in the authentic Pauline letters there are passages that seem to
be interpolations — material added to a document by another
hand. Scholars have their own methods of making these
determinations, including a close study of the vocabulary and
usage of the writer, and comparisons between different
versions of the texts themselves. It is not enough, however,

to account for a passage as an interpolation. The passage itself still requires our respectful attention to what it is actually saying and to whom. But it should not be used to interpret the mind of an author if he did not write it.

When we look at what remains as undeniably from Paul's own pen, we try to see Paul in his circumstances. For the purposes of this book, we are looking for what the epistles tell us about some of his basic theological insights. We are primarily interested in his understanding of Genesis 1:26-28 as it concerns the creation of humankind, male and female, in the image and likeness of God. We are looking especially at the ways that Paul tried, and we try in our time, to interpret the Genesis text in the context of his life setting and in relationship to the questions and problems of the first Christian communities, his audience.

I read the Bible as a record of how the people of God understood their own experience. I read Paul as a friend, a struggling Christian like me, made of flesh and blood, with cultural and personal limitations, obsessions perhaps, as well as enthusiasms, hopes and visions. Unlike me, he was an adult convert to Christianity, deeply rooted in the faith of the Hebrew scriptures, and called by God to accept a new revelation of the divine in Jesus the Christ, an experience that puzzled him deeply and challenged his dearest prejudices and certainties. He had to give up a mature, unified religious belief and practice to accept the lordship of Jesus.

At this point I recall an incident in the chapel of our mother house during the celebration of the Unity Octave, when Christians and Jews had come together for prayer. A Protestant speaker had implied that we are all far away from God until we find God through Christ. A rabbi who followed him draped himself over the lectern and said, slowly, deliberately, lovingly, without tension or hostility, "I don't feel far from God. I feel *close* to God."

I too feel that believing Jews are close to God, and that God's promises to them, and the revelation of divine justice and love which God has given us all through them, are real and true. I love Paul for struggling so with this issue — for wanting to be *lost* if his people might be saved. I do not know how to solve any of the questions raised by Christian/Jewish dialogue. I hold onto two apparently incompatible concepts: the election of the Jews, and the redemption wrought through the death and resurrection of a Jewish messiah.

When I read Paul's letters, I look not only for specific teaching about specific issues, which is important, but chiefly for his broad perspectives, his deep insights, and his sense of the *crux* of things — where the cross is in our experience. Most of all I look for his groping after the vision of a new creation in which Jew and Greek, male and female, bond and free, are united in one community of love and faith in the Son and Servant of God, the risen Jesus.

In talking about some of the New Testament material that relates to the theme of creation of female and male in the image and likeness of God, I shall begin with the writings of Paul. Then I will look at what some passages from the Gospels show us about the words, actions, and attitudes of Jesus, and conclude with some reflections about Mary, the mother of Jesus.

The Hebrew scriptures furnish us with three great theological themes about creation: what God made, what happened to it, and what God promised. In the Old Testament the words "image" and "likeness" are closely related in meaning, and together they say that human beings are like God, reflect God's character, and *are not* God. One aspect of the image and likeness is dominion over the rest of creation. The result of the Fall is the distortion of this image, a distortion reflected in the experience of suffering, toil and death, and the disfigurement of the garden in the rank growth of thorns and weeds. The promise of a new creation is hinted at in the story of the flood and the sign of the rainbow, which pointed to God's mercy in reversing judgment upon human sin and to the establishment of the covenant.

In Paul's writings these themes are restated in terms of the language and culture of his day, and transformed as he develops his theology in the light of his own conversion when he encountered the risen Jesus, and his subsequent life in the church.

Before we consider Paul's teaching in some detail, we need to look more closely at the religious and cultural context of his life. When the Christian gospel entered the wider culture of the Graeco-Roman world which surrounded it, one dominated by Greek philosophy, language, and religion, overlaid by the order and administrative genius of Rome, it came into contact with a world view different from that of its Hebrew origins. The interaction between the first Christian preaching on the one hand, and Hellenistic thought forms, vocabulary and categories of interpretation on the other, shaped the Christian scriptures, including the letters of Paul.

This interaction between the Christian proclamation of the lordship of Jesus and contemporary religious and social attitudes also created some new models for holiness for individuals and for communities. It also produced ambiguities, contradictions and surprises. We shall see both in the examples from the literature of the New Testament. In the communities of the first Christians, as we hear about them in the letters of Paul, how was the theology of the image of God in us understood?

In his writings Paul uses both "image" and "likeness" to refer to Christ as the image of the Father, and to us as partakers of the same image through our incorporation into Christ. A passage in Philippians 2:6-11 speaks of Jesus as being "in the form (*morphé*) of God" (v. 6), suggesting a copy or image; the visible likeness to God, put aside in the self-emptying of the Son, was restored by God at the resurrection (vv. 7-9). In II Corinthians 4:4 Paul speaks of "the light of the gospel of the glory of Christ, who is the likeness (*eikon*) of God," while the same epistle states that "we all...are being changed into his likeness (*eikon*) from one degree of glory to another" (3:18).

With I Corinthians we have another passage that shows the relationship, in the mind of Paul, of the image of God in Christ and our participation in the same image. The first human being, "*anthropos*," Adam, is alive by the gift of God but also destined to die as the "man of dust" (15:47). Christ is the second Adam, not of dust but of heaven, and we are connected to both the first and second Adam: "Just as we have borne the image of the man of dust, we shall bear also the image of the man of heaven" (v. 49). These verses of I Corinthians 15 are part of Paul's great writing on the resurrection of the body.

Paul's teaching about the Fall also uses the themes of image and likeness. In II Corinthians 3:12-17 he describes fallenness in terms of a veil which obscures the reflected glory of God's face, and in I Corinthians 13:12 he speaks of the distorted image which is reflected in a mirror. Mirrors in Paul's day were made of polished metal, a substance which can reflect images dimly, but without the precision and brilliance of the looking-glasses of our day. The veil and the dull mirror describe our fallen condition. As the corporate body of Christ, and in our individual lives, we still bear some dim traces of our heavenly origin and destiny, but we do not yet reveal clearly the new creation. Christ is in us as the hope of a glory to come.

Yet it is not our suffering, humiliations and failure that distort the image of Christ in us; on the contrary, they reveal the image of the crucified and risen Lord (II Cor. 4:7-12). The cross of Christ appears to those without faith as abasement and slavery (Phil. 2:7) or folly and scandal (I Cor. 1:18, 22-25). For Paul, however, the cross is also glory, wisdom and the salvation of the world (Phil. 2:9-11; I Cor. 1:24; Rom. 1:16; Gal. 1:4). He identifies his own experience of abasement, humiliation, disappointment and bodily suffering with the cross of Jesus. He speaks of his grief and

sense of failure over the blindness and hardness of heart of
his early converts and his burden of responsibility for the
churches, and gives us that vigorous, precise list of his
sufferings at the hands of the authorities of both church and
state (II Cor. 11:23-30).

Paul also gives us an image of hope through the
metaphor of a seed: "What you sow does not come to life
unless it dies" (I Cor. 15:36). "What is sown is perishable" —
like our frail flesh — "what is raised is imperishable" — our
real life in God. "It is sown in dishonor" — as we are in our
failures, fears, and anxieties — "it is raised in glory" — as we
are destined to be. We are made in the image of God and we
never lose that image. It is obscured from us by our unbelief
and sin, and because we live in time. The glory of the
kingdom fully come is in the future. Then the image and
likeness will be fully revealed to us.

As we are all members of Christ's body, so too the
Christian community is constituted by its oneness in Christ
and reflects his image: "For as many of you as were
baptized into Christ have put on Christ." This oneness
transcends social and sexual divisions: "There is neither Jew
nor Greek, there is neither slave nor free, there is neither
male nor female; for you are all one in Christ Jesus.... For
neither circumcision counts for anything, nor uncircumcision,
but a new creation" (Gal. 3:27-8; 6:15). According to Paul,
the qualities that mark the church as a "new creation"
include mutuality, servanthood, the primacy of love, and
freedom from guilt and the fear of death.

Mutuality is expressed in exhortations such as "Let no
one seek his own good, but the good of his neighbors," and
"Now there are varieties of gifts, but the same Spirit....To
each is given the manifestation of the Spirit for the common
good" (I Cor. 10:24; 12:4,7).

Servanthood is expressed in figurative language about the
body and its members in mutual service to each other, "that
there may be no discord in the body, but that the members
may have the same care for one another" (I Cor. 12:35). In

[31]

thinking about Paul's theology of community, we must bear
in mind that his writings are not systematic nor didactic, but
responses to concrete situations. He cared about the
churches, the little groups of Christians he had fathered, and
Paul takes with deep seriousness the specific problems and
questions that are referred to him. His replies are practical
as well as theological; they are not idealistic, nor are they
designed to become building blocks for a theological system.
The letters seem to be tiny points of entrance to the glory
beyond, pinpricks in the veil of history through which we
glimpse the kingdom.

"Now you are the body of Christ," Paul says, and God
has appointed a ministry of leadership and healing unequally:
"Are all apostles? Are all prophets? Are all teachers? Do
all work miracles? Do all possess the gifts of healing? Do
all speak with tongues? Do all interpret?" (I Cor. 12:29-30)
Paul thinks of the Christian churches as communities that
include friends, coworkers, both women and men, the newly-
baptized, slaves, freed or not, the married and the unmarried,
widows and virgins. He speaks to them all as "sanctified in
Christ Jesus, called to be saints together with all those who in
every place call on the name of our Lord Jesus Christ" (I
Cor. 1:2). Paul recognizes their gifts and is thankful for their
"partnership in the gospel" (Phil. 1:5). He also makes no
bones about rebuking them: "Finally, brethren, farewell.
Mend your ways, heed my appeal, agree with one another,
live in peace and the God of love and peace be with you" (II
Cor. 13:11). Is it not fair to assume that he included
"sisters"?

Paul has a bad name in many quarters for his attitude to
women and marriage. Indeed, passages from his writings
have often been used to reinforce the idea that Christians
believe it is God's will for women to be subordinate to men.
When we look at his writings, there is some justification for
his reputation, but we have also seen strong currents in his
thought which lead to a different interpretation and
evaluation. Is he consistent?

There is no doubt, for example, that in I Corinthians Paul recommends celibacy over marriage (7:1-9). In the same passage, however, he introduces a radically new teaching when he says, "For the wife does not rule over her own body, but the husband does," but then goes on to add, "Likewise the husband does not rule over his own body, but the wife does" (v. 4). This is neither Jewish nor Greek nor Roman, it is Christian spirituality according to Paul — an idea of marriage as mutual partnership.

He seems also to have accepted women along with men in sharing his own apostolic labors. In Romans 16:1 Paul commends "our sister Phoebe, a deaconess of the church at Cenchreae, that you may receive her in the Lord as befits the saints, and help her in whatsoever she may require from you, for she has been a helper of many and of myself as well. Greet Prisca and Aquila, my fellow workers in Christ Jesus." We notice that, contrary to the custom of his day, Paul names Prisca before her husband, Aquila. In Romans 16:7 he also speaks of Andronicus and Junia as a missionary team, a man and woman who were both acknowledged as apostles.[5]

When we recall Paul's baptismal statement — "For as many of you as were baptized into Christ, have put on Christ. There is neither Jew nor Greek, there is neither slave nor free. There is neither male nor female; for you are all one in Christ Jesus" (Gal. 3:27-8) — we seem to have a theological basis for the acceptance of women and men as equals in the church, and fellow laborers in his missionary enterprise. On the other hand, we have the puzzling passage from I Corinthians 11:2-16 which asserts that Christ is the head of every man and the husband is the head of every woman, as well as the directive that every woman must be veiled when she prays or prophesies. Men, on the contrary, are to pray and prophesy with head uncovered. Paul's reason? "For a man ought not to cover his head, since he is the image and glory of God, but woman is the glory of man." Here women are not said to be in the image of God.

Some commentators argue that Paul is speaking only of married women here, and that the passage is an interpretation of the J creation story; it is intended not to prohibit women from leading worship in the church, but to regulate the way in which they, as distinct from men, should dress when doing so. Others point out that "head" (*kephalé*) can be translated as "source." The whole passage then becomes an early Christian commentary upon Genesis 2:21-3, referring to the creation of woman from the flesh of man.

Others maintain that this passage in I Corinthians is an interpolation, or a series of interpolations. The arguments against its being from Paul's own hand include the following points. Nowhere else does Paul concern himself with details of clothing and dress. Furthermore, the whole passage could be omitted without disturbing the context or flow: the transition from 11:2 to 11:17 is smooth and logical. Nowhere else does Paul speak of the feminine as subordinate. The passage is not in agreement with Galatians 3:28, which is genuinely from Paul, nor with Paul's view of his fellow workers in Romans 16.

Still more puzzling is the provision in I Corinthians 14:33-35: "As in all the church of the saints, the women should keep silence in the churches. For they are not permitted to speak, but should be subordinate, even as the law says." Why provide for women to pray and prophesy with veiled heads, and then forbid them to speak at all in the churches? The passage is generally thought to be an interpolation, and not a genuine statement by Paul, for two reasons. Paul did not speak of the "churches of the saints." This is terminology of a more developed stage of church polity. Nor does he usually refer to the law as a Christian standard, holding rather that a man is justified by faith, apart from work or the law (Rom. 3:28, and, of course, in many other places).

The further belief that women share the guilt of Eve and hence are punishable has darkened the lives of many women through the two millenia of Christian history. Is this the

teaching of Paul? In Romans 5:12, he says, "Therefore, as
sin came into the world through one man and death through
sin, so death spread to all men because all men sinned." Paul
attributes the entrance of sin into the world not to the
woman, as the later church was to do so often (a conclusion
which justified and continued much social injustice against
women in succeeding ages), but to "one man," that is, one
human being (*anthropos*).

The letters to the Corinthian communities in particular
must be understood in the specific context of Paul's own
concerns and in the light of the questions he was trying to
answer and the dangers he was trying to guard against, on
behalf of the Christian church he was responsible for. He
seems to have stood neither with those who tried to retain the
common assumptions about women current among the Jews
of Palestine and in the Diaspora, that the woman is inferior
and subordinate to the man, nor with the Gnostic Christians,
who wanted to eliminate altogether the social and cultic
distinctions between men and women.[6] It is also evident that
Paul was not, in his lifetime, able to apply his own insights
beyond individuals to social classes. It seems to me that no
one could have done that in the thought-world of his day,
when the concept of social class structure was so little
developed.

It is not enough to oppose Pauline and non-Pauline
material without asking for the reason for interpolations, as
well as their meaning and value. The interpolations we have
discussed, as well as the writings attributed to Paul but
coming from a later time and a different hand, reflect
concerns about marriage, sexuality and women which are
more strongly influenced by traditional Jewish and early
Christian materials than Paul was. More interested in the
church as a community to be built up in love, and in the
success of his missionary work, he reinterpreted social and
cultural values more profoundly than the later, more cautious
and conservative writers of Ephesians, Colossians and I
Timothy, with their "household codes," lists of requirements

for the proper behavior of classes of people such as women, wives, children and slaves. Paul's vision of the church as a community of equals and his bold summing up of that vision in Galatians 3:27-28, represented a radical equality of all persons in Christ which did not deeply modify the patriarchal attitudes of later writers.

Christians, women and men alike, shared through their oneness with Christ, whom Paul described as the image (*eikon*) of God, in the ministry of giftedness. Both took part in the missionary enterprise and upbuilding of the church as the body of Christ, both received the supreme gift of love for each other, and both partook of the common meal of the Eucharist.

It is inconsistent with this Pauline vision to exclude a woman from ministry, to assign primacy of guilt to her, and to suggest that for her, salvation comes, not from faith in the redeeming work of Christ, but "through bearing children" (I Tim. 2:15)! We can recognize that I Timothy is not by Paul and fails to reach the heights of the genuine Pauline epistles. It comes from a different, and later, period, by another author.

As a teacher of mine once pointed out, there are basically two ways to deal with intrapersonal conflict — the dividedness we all feel from time to time between our highest aspirations and most compelling visions of holiness on the one hand, and the reality of our limitations, weaknesses and sinfulness on the other. One is to level down our aspirations and to correct, to a reasonable degree, our weaknesses and our erroneous perceptions of ourselves. The price we pay for the resulting relative peace of mind is the loss of the high points of spiritual experience. The other way is to accept ambiguity and inconsistency in ourselves, and to hang onto the highest vision in spite of the discomfort and despair to which it opens us.

If we require Paul at all times and in all circumstances to live up to his greatest moments of inspiration and his openness to the vision God gave him for the church, we shall

have to explain away what seems to us his lapses into
attitudes of mind toward women, toward slaves, and toward
authority, which do not seem to be consistent with this
vision. Paul's own view of himself in Romans reflects his
sense of brokenness: "For I delight in the law of God in my
inmost self, but I see in my members another law at war with
the law of my mind and making me captive to the law of sin
which dwells in my members. Wretched man that I am, who
shall deliver me from this body of death?" (Rom 7:23-24)

We can, on the contrary, accept Paul as a brother in
Christ, struggling as we all do, to discern God's will and plan
for us in the society, family, culture and personal vocation
God has given each one of us. He seems to me to be a sign
and channel for the love and healing grace of God when he
speaks about the great gift of Christ, the work of the Spirit,
the reality of our incorporation into Christ, and the primacy
of merciful, humble, genuine love for each other. When he
tries to apply his vision to specific cultural details, like
women's dress in church (if indeed he does), or when he
deals with the oppressed classes of his day — women,
children and slaves — he seems to have left for us some
further work to do. He has not exhausted the meaning of
community as a new creation, as the body of Christ who is
the image of God.

Now we have seen something of how Paul recognized
that Christ was the image of God and that we ourselves,
women and men, baptized into Christ, share that image
without distinction as to sex. We have also seen how he
understood the Christian community as persons bound
together in one love, the love of Christ.

We must come now to the heart of it all — to Jesus.
What does Jesus show us about ourselves, men and women, in
the image and likeness of God? What does he teach us about
our responsibility for the earth and for each other? How
does he deal with women and men? Does Jesus seem to

value feminine qualities equally with masculine ones? How far did he accommodate himself to the patriarchal language and culture of his own people? How can women today relate to a male savior? I shall use material from all four gospels as signs pointing toward Jesus in order to try to see how they speak to us about these questions, without trying to separate the different levels of tradition.

As to the verse in Genesis about our creation in the image and likeness of God, Jesus makes no reference to it. He uses "image" only in the story of the question about paying taxes to Caesar, when he asks of the coin shown him: "Whose image (*eikon*) and superscription is this?" (Mt. 12:16). The implication of the story is that the image is linked to its prototype.

In the parables of the kingdom, he gives us fresh images, homely similes for the kingdom into which we are called, men and women alike. It is like a net, or a bit of leaven in the hands of a woman, a mustard seed, a hidden treasure, a pearl — similes which spring, as all wisdom literature does, from the experiences of small, ordinary folk intent on providing for their families and cultivating their gardens. These similes are in contrast to the apocalyptic descriptions of the coming of the kingdom like a thief in the night, like the rolling up of a scroll, like the lightning from east to west.

Our likeness to God is revealed in these similes. The kingdom is *for* us — it fits us and we are fitted for it. It is both hidden and revealed; both here and now, and in the future; both quiet and crashingly noisy. We are so made that small things show us God, and our smallness is not the last word. Our experience is subject also to cataclysms of revelation, when new and larger perspectives are forced upon us. God's revelation can be expressed in a nudge or a whisper, in a thunderclap or a burst of incredible light. We are made for both, for the small and the great; in the kingdom the last shall be first and the first, last.

In the Priestly version of the Genesis creation story, the first human pair is given responsibility for the welfare of the rest of creation. They are to have dominion, to "till the earth and subdue it." In the "J" version they are to "till it and keep it." This has sometimes been interpreted as setting humanity over the rest of creation as its lord. Jesus, however, did not look kindly on his disciples' desire for ascendancy. "The kings of the Gentiles exercise lordship....But not so with you; rather let the greatest among you become as the youngest, and the leader as one who serves...I am among you as one who serves" (Lk. 22:25-7). What could be plainer? The Fourth Gospel tells a story about Jesus that says the same thing. At a solemn moment Jesus, knowing that these were his final hours, at table with his disciples for the last time, took a towel and washed their feet. Afterwards he said: "If I then, your Lord and Teacher, have washed your feet, you ought also to wash one another's feet" (Jn. 13:14). Jesus overturns all our ideas of lordship in these two stories. The only mode of leadership for a disciple of Jesus is humble service.

Paul's conception of baptism was that through it we die with Christ and rise again in newness of life. His statement in Galatians that in Christ there is neither male nor female seems to me to have formed itself through his experience of the first Christian churches, in Antioch especially (Acts 11:19-26). While we may look in vain in the gospels for any statement maintaining in principle the equality of men and women, Jesus' attitude toward women was the same as his attitude toward men — in itself a revolutionary stance in first-century Palestine. The stories the early church collected and told about him show that his attitude was realistic, discriminating and perceptive, loving, compassionate, attentive and fearless. The stories in the gospels are richly diversified in their descriptions of individual men and women, and he does not stereotype women or men. He gave no special rules for women, slaves or children. There is no sign of a tendency to disparage women, much less to blame or curse them. On the contrary, discipleship, apostleship and the kingdom were open to them. Luke 8:1-3 shows that women were with the twelve, preaching and bringing good news, and Matthew 28:7 has women announcing the resurrection to the rest of the disciples. To be a witness of the resurrection was the mark of an apostle.

Two stories about women and two about men show how similar Jesus' response was to both sexes, and how free he was both from fear of the cultural prejudices of his day and from the need to stereotype women.

The first example is the story of the barren woman (Mark 12:18-27). Jesus is approached by the Sadducees and asked a catch question about the resurrection. A woman has married seven brothers in succession, as each one in turn died and left her no children. "In the resurrection, whose wife will she be? For each one had her." It is a grotesque story, in which the woman has no more identity than a farm animal, useful only for reproduction. She is a mute figure, serving not only seven husbands in succession in their vain pursuit of family continuity, but also serving the men who told the story to make a point.

Jesus' reply lifts the argument to another plane altogether. He gives a judgment on this trumped-up case: "You are wrong," he says. You neither understand the Scripture nor the power of God when you try to reason about the life to come as if it were subject to all the limitations of our present life. In the life to come, men and women will not be divided by sex. They are "like angels in heaven." However we may understand angels, traditionally they are thought to be messengers of God, ministering spirits, helpers of the dying. They are not divided into two sexes and they bear no children. For Jesus the woman is not defined by her sexuality, nor is she judged by her inability to bear children. He has revalued the barren woman, and seen her in the light of the kingdom into which she has been invited.

Jesus does two things in this story. He rescues a barren woman from social stigma and he refutes an argument about resurrection. He is attentive to the woman's possibilities, compassionate toward her situation, and he suggests to his

questioners a very different evaluation from theirs: her
worth is the same as their own.

In the Fourth Gospel there is a story about a poor,
friendless man, blind, lame and paralyzed, among a crowd of
invalids around a pool which was reputed to have a healing
power. "When Jesus saw him and knew he had been lying
there a long time, he said to him, 'Do you want to be
healed?'" A tremendous question to put to a person in such
a case. "The sick man answered him, 'Sir, I have no man to
put me into the pool when the water is troubled, and while I
am going, another steps down before me.'" Jesus healed him,
by-passing the pool: "'Rise, take up your pallet, and walk'"
(John 5:2-9). Looking along the trajectory of the Fourth
Gospel, we see the same figure of Jesus that we saw in
Luke's gospel, attentive, responsive, discriminating, decisive.
The man had been ill a long time, and he had no friend.
Jesus befriended him. In the second half of this story, John
5:9b-15, we see again the man Jesus healed by the pool. The
Jews have questioned him about his bodily healing, but Jesus
confronts him about the state of his soul. " 'See, you are
well! Sin no more, that nothing worse befall you.' " Here
sin is recognized, confronted, and forgiven. In both stories, a
woman and a man are set free. Many other stories in the
gospels point to the same Jesus as a friend of sinners and a
healer of both men and women.

Two other stories have to do with Jesus' attitude toward
the poor. In the story about the widow's mite (Mk. 13:41-4),
Jesus observes a poor widow who makes her small offering
for the Temple: "Truly I say to you, this poor widow has
put in more than all those who are contributing to the
treasury, for they all contributed out of their abundance, but
she out of her poverty has put in everything she had, her
whole living." This remark is usually understood as praise
for the woman and for her generosity in giving to the
church, but it can equally well be interpreted as a lament and
a rebuke to the rich. The religious establishment enriches
itself at the expense of the poor, and the widow's two copper

coins are more than the offering of the rich, who do not give proportionately. Jesus again notices an individual woman, takes account of her circumstances, acknowledges her reality, values her sacrifice.

The story of the rich young ruler (Mk. 10:17-31; Mt. 19:16-30; Lk. 18:18-30) is also about the question of poverty and riches. In response to the question, "What must I do to inherit eternal life?" a rich man is first told by Jesus to keep the commandments. Upon hearing his reply, "All these I have observed from my youth," Jesus looked upon him, loved him, and said to him, " 'You lack one thing: go, sell what you have and give to the poor and you will have treasure in heaven; and come, follow me.' " And the young man went away sorrowful. He could not bring himself to part with his great possessions.

Both stories deal with poverty. The woman and the man are individuals and their circumstances are different. The sacrifice of the poor widow is recognized, while the rich man is loved, challenged and allowed to refuse. In both stories poverty is an evil we are called to alleviate.

Jesus dealt even-handedly with women and with men. He numbered both among his friends and disciples, and he confronted and forgave sinners of both sexes. We do not know what stories about Jesus Paul knew, nor what access he had to the earliest traditions about Jesus, but his own vision of the Christian community in which there are "neither Jew nor Greek, bond nor free, male nor female" is concordant with the picture we receive in the gospels of Jesus' treatment of men and women. It has often been noted that Jesus disregarded many of the taboos of his religion, especially those which oppressed women, or which would have prevented him from reaching out to help people in need.

In the fourth chapter of the Gospel of John there is the story about a woman who, from the Jewish point of view, was triply cursed — because she was a woman, because she was a Samaritan with a false belief, and because she was unclean. No respectable rabbi would speak to a woman in public, certainly not to a Samaritan woman. Jesus, however, in this story disregards all of these taboos and not only speaks to her, but asks her for a drink of water. Cleanness and uncleanness seem to mean nothing to him. Instead he asks a favor of her and receives what she has to give. In return, Jesus speaks to her of "living water" he will give and which will become the spring of living water welling up to eternal life. He makes her his follower: "So the woman left her water jar, and went away to the city, and said to the people, 'Come, see a man who told me all that I ever did. Can this be the Christ?'" (Jn. 4:28-9).

In the story of the widow's son (Lk. 7:11-17) Jesus reaches out his hands to touch the defiling bier on which a young man lies dead. Jesus touches that bier and heals and raises the dead man. In this story two things strike me. First, Jesus is moved, he is acted upon powerfully when he sees the bereaved woman. He shows anger and compassion, two feelings close together and sometimes expressed by the same word in Greek. In the second part of the story, he is active; he puts out his hand to the bier. He has moved into the sphere of uncleanness, the sphere of death. For a Jew, as for many ancient people, the dead body was unclean, contaminating, contagious. Jesus' action complements his compassion. Together they are life-giving: "And he gave him to his mother." Compassion without action can be sentimentality. Action without compassion is aggression. It is only when the two come together that something whole is given. It is not an easy business trying to hold them together. We are all tempted to do one or the other, to overbalance one by the other. But wholeness consists of both together, action and compassion, in mutuality.

Jesus' response to all classes is compassionate and respectful. He speaks words of blessing to the sick, the adulterous, the harlot, the barren, the virgin and the widow, and deals gently with the poor and with the rich young ruler. This kind of response on Jesus' part is in keeping with the saying recorded by both Matthew and Luke in which he says

of himself: " 'O Jerusalem....How often I would have
gathered your children together as a hen gathers her brood
under her wings, and you would not!' " (Lk. 13:34; Mt. 23:37)

Obviously a predominant quality of Scripture is its use of
masculine qualities and masculine language in describing God
— a mighty warrior, a king, a judge — even though feminine
images sometimes exist alongside them. For example the
Hebrew word for "womb," *rechem*, is sometimes used to
describe God's compassionate "motherly love," or "womb
love." In Isaiah 42:14 God is described as being like a
woman in travail. Yet as Rosemary Ruether warns us in
Sexism and God Talk, we do not solve the problem of gender
stereotyping on the level of God-language by including the
feminine side of God in a male hierarchy.[7] She points to
elements in Scripture that tend to overturn the hierarchy
itself: God liberated the enslaved Hebrews, and their earliest
political structure was not a monarchy, but a tribal
confederation. We cannot, I think, escape from the
patriarchal or androcentric vocabulary of the Bible where
God is Father, Priest and King, but we can see clearly how
Jesus upsets hierarchy and reinterprets dominion as humble
service, in his own example of obedience unto the death of a
slave, as well as in his words, "Be not lords over each other."

However we may solve the problem of translating the
patriarchal language of our scriptures and liturgies, the
original texts will remain, with the marks of their cultural
origin upon them. Personal devotion may require us to begin
praying to God as Mother, Nurturer, Pain-bearer, and to
read "she" for "he" in the liturgy. Some women are no
longer able to accept a male savior and look instead for a
goddess figure.

Rosemary Ruether believes that it does not do to elevate
the feminine qualities of God and of Christ, since this will
force women into "specializing in the representation of the
feminine," which means exclusion from the exercise of the
roles of power and leadership associated with masculinity.
She asks whether the maleness of Christ forces women to

conclude that he can no longer represent any redemptive possibility for women as persons. Ruether's preferred Christology is the Christ of liberation theology. She sees Jesus as liberator of the oppressed, including women: "His ability to speak as liberator does not reside in his maleness, but in the fact that he has renounced this system of domination and seeks to embody in his person the new humanity of service and mutual empowerment." She can see the Christ figure as our redeemer only if we do not regard the historical Incarnation as encapsulated in Jesus once and for all. "The Christian community continues Christ's identity...we can encounter Christ in the form of our sister." Why not? Where else, for many of us? And the redeemed community is "not only women, but a new humanity, female and male."[8]

Patricia Wilson-Kastner sees the limiting specifics of Jesus, his sex, state of knowledge, racial origin and place in time, as examples of "God's humility and self-emptying in living among us. Jesus became flesh so as to show forth the love of God among us, a love which is not merely the expression of good will, but the power of an energy which is the heart, core and cohesive force of the universe."[9]

Finally, we cannot talk about images of the feminine in the New Testament without talking about Mary, the mother of Jesus. "The Blessed Virgin Mary" calls up a vast array of theological complications, iconographic proliferation, and liturgical developments. She has also called forth dogmatic statements; in 1950 we had the papal decree of the dogma of Mary's Assumption, a decree that Carl Jung claimed promoted Mary into the Godhead and indeed made her a fourth member of a divine quadernity. Her titles are legion and her image is everywhere in Christianity, especially in Eastern Orthodox, Roman Catholic and Anglican churches and religious houses, and in many a devout household the world over.

One of the few references to her virginity in the post-apostolic church is from Ignatius of Antioch in his *Epistle to* the Ephesians, 19: "Now the virginity of Mary was hidden from the prince of this world, as was also her offspring, and the death of the Lord; three mysteries of renown which were wrought in silence." It might have been better if she had indeed been left in the mystery of silence, but she has not.

Her basic title is God-bearer, *Theotokos*. This title is Christological, not Mariological and certainly not ascetical. She is not a pattern for feminine chastity. She is instead a poor woman, and that is the point of her virginity in the birth narratives of Matthew and Luke. Her story points toward a characteristic of the work of God, one named in the *Magnificat*: he lifts up the poor, the oppressed, the humble and the helpless. His choice of Mary for the work of the redemption is in keeping with his choice of the small, unimportant group of Hebrew nomads to be his chosen people, his calling them out of Egypt and bestowal of the Promised Land, and all the other promises, constantly renewed, that they are his people and that from them salvation for the world will come.

Several currents seem to have converged upon Mary to create a complex figure of purity and power, and to produce a Mariology that stresses her separation from normal sexual life. Not only was the conception of Jesus virginal, so was his birth in later legendary development. Mary was never a real wife to Joseph. The ascetical trend in Christianity was strengthened when it was introduced into the Hellenistic world with its dualism of flesh and spirit, and the elevation of one over the other. The result was the image of a woman who was exalted because of her distance from passion and from feeling, conjugal love and ordinary family life. She becomes an object lesson for women, a model of propriety, humility, domesticity, and purity.

Another trend exalted Mary as intercessor, more merciful than either Jesus or God the Father, and gave her titles such as *Mediatrix*, Mother of Mercy, Queen of Heaven, of Africa, of the New World, of Peace, of Victory, and so on.

We have noted the figure of a woman in the Book of
Revelation clothed with the sun, her feet on the moon and
crowned with stars; originally this figure denoted Israel as the
mother of the Messiah and the church as the New Jerusalem,
and *not* Mary, the historical mother of Jesus. Only in the
third and fourth centuries is the woman understood as Mary.
Her promotion to the status of ever-virgin and queen seems
to have been activated by popular devotion more than by
dogmatic development. Very early, liturgical hymns and
antiphons elaborate on her beauty and purity and power. As
the development of the devotion to Jesus tended to downplay
and obscure the reality and limitations of his human flesh
and history, so his mother was removed from her identity as
a Jewish peasant woman who had a baby with a dread
destiny, who bore him in a humble place, followed him with
other disciples, misunderstood his vocation, was rebuked and
instructed by him and stood by him at his terrible end —
stood, not swooned, as some pictures of her show — who
never saw him again as far as the gospels are concerned, and
whose last appearance in the Bible is in the upper room with
the other disciples, waiting.

As Jesus is exalted into the heavenly sphere, his mother
shares his noble estate. He becomes Lord and she becomes
Lady, Our Lady. As the Church waxes powerful in the
world, seeks dominion and claims infallibility, so Mary grows
in power, becoming in popular imagination the intercessor
who alone is able to intervene between the sinner and an
avenging God. I wish she had been left hidden in silence.

When I look through the various perspectives of
Scripture, the nativity stories of Luke and Matthew, the
gospel of John, when I consider how both Paul and Mark are
silent about her, I am struck by how much silence there is.
Ignatius is right. She is the woman hidden in silence, clothed
in silence, not clothed with the sun or the moon. She is
clothed in ordinariness and dailiness. I see her as a poor
woman, a virgin, incomplete, one of the faithful remnant of
Israel, waiting for the promise of God and chosen to be the

mother of the Messiah. To the announcement by an angel, her response is a challenge. How can this be? The angelic reply is that God's intervention in the processes of human life will bring conception and birth. The Spirit alone brings her to fullness and maturity.

In Luke's gospel Mary calls herself *doule*, handmaid, one who cooperates with God in redemption. She is chosen by God and overshadowed by the Spirit, and the *Magnificat* is put into her mouth. Mark interprets her differently. In an episode from Mark's gospel she is not a faithful disciple of Jesus, but rather joins with "his brothers" and with those of his friends who think he is mad and try to take him away from his ministry (Mk. 3:21. 33-5).

We see Mary at the marriage at Cana in John's gospel, not understanding. Her command, "Do whatever he tells you," exalts Jesus' sovereignty rather than her own intervention, although much pious speculation has developed around this scene (Jn. 2:5). John, like Mark and Paul, omits all mention of the virgin birth. In the Fourth Gospel Mary is the personification of Israel as the people of God. Mary at the foot of the cross is not Mary as an individual woman, the mother of all Christians; rather it is the church that is the mother of all Christians. The figure of Mary as an "icon of the church" is a later theological development, and the New Testament does not present her this way.

I have my own image of Mary, the mother of Jesus. I see her as a youngish woman, sturdy in build, with short dark hair, a little curly, and a trim figure that is neither thin nor delicate. I see her joining a group, putting out her arms and taking the hands of the persons next to her, entering a circle, joining a dance. It is a slow dance, neither solemn nor merry, but graceful, and lively and joyous. She is the kind of woman one would like to have on one's side at such times as an emergency, the sudden arrival of unexpected guests who need food and beds, or a tough moment during a political demonstration when the police bear down with tear gas and dogs. I do not see this figure very clearly. It is as if she is obscured by a little dust or a mist or a gentle storm of rain. I look through it. I suppose this part of my image comes from the fact that we can look toward Mary only through the eyes of different people who have seen her in different ways and recorded what they saw. There is no way to bring her into clear focus and yet I have a sense that all of us are looking at one and the same woman, and that she is real, fleshly, Jewish, a mother and a wife. Is she also the woman clothed with the sun? I can perhaps understand this. Her beauty and power, her radiance, is the shining out of ordinary daily generosity, friendliness, self-giving love, well symbolized by the sun. I can understand why the moon is at her feet. She is a woman and the moon is a woman's symbol. It seems right also that she should be crowned with twelve stars because she is a Jewish woman and springs from one of the twelve tribes of Israel and because the child she bore is the promised redeemer, the Messiah of all Israel.

She is still the woman wrapped in silence and mystery, and I am content to leave her there as far as doctrines are concerned. I do not know where she is buried or whether she is buried. I do not know the circumstances of her conception. I believe that she bore a child in the normal way. How the child was conceived, I do not know. Scripture says that the child to be born of her would be called Emmanuel, God with us, and I believe that, too. And it is enough.

The Chariot and the Banquet

In the sixteenth century Richard Hooker gave Anglicans a threefold criterion of authority which has endured the test of time. He looked for a middle way between the claims of papal authority and the Puritan principle of "scripture alone." He offers us a synthesis of three strands: Scripture, tradition and reason. Through them the supreme authority of God as he is revealed in Christ speaks to the Christian mind, conscience and affections. Scripture, as the account of how the people of God understood their history, is the primary source of authority. It was the Christian community speaking as the church that determined which books belonged in the Bible, and closed the canon.

Tradition, on the other hand, includes Christian literature of many kinds: hymns, commentaries, sermons and treatises, canon law and liturgy, poetry and devotional works. It serves to interpret Scripture and give guidance to a growing community of the faithful. Ideally, in the long run, tradition is ratified through consensus. While the words of Scripture are fixed and may not be altered, tradition is free-flowing, innovative, interpretive and critical. It includes in its grab-bag wonderfully imaginative arabesques, fancy and sober criticism, theological analysis, both sober and extravagant. Some of it eventually falls by its own weight of silliness or perversity, but some abides from century to century.

Without a fixed canon, I suppose the biblical message would have been obscured by the distortions of partisan theology, prejudice, pedantry, the tendency of hagiography to present every event and every individual as either perfectly holy or perfectly satanic. Tradition, together with

[50]

Scripture and the conscientious reason and sense of general
rightness which each individual has to some extent, forms for
Anglicans the famous three-legged stool of our theory of
authority. It can be described as an evasion, a watering-
down of the stern claims of the Bible, or as an opening of
the door to something our Roman Catholic critics used to
refer to, not without scorn, as "private judgment." Our
attitude to our tradition can also be looked upon as an
example of typically British "muddling through," but I think
it has served us well.

Reading the Christian classics which are part of our
inherited tradition requires of us some effort to relate them
to Scripture, and to use our own judgment as to what we
accept and what we reject. We are not bound to believe
everything that any of our authors says. In this book we are
considering especially Gregory of Nyssa, Augustine of Hippo,
Dante Alighieri, and Julian of Norwich, as representing
tradition in the early and medieval periods. We shall be
looking at what these four have to say about the image of
God in us and what new metaphors they may give us for the
meeting of God with human persons, and our meetings with
one another. We shall also be alert to read them critically,
and to assess how far they seem to speak for God and for the
Christian church, and where they may have gone astray.

This is a somewhat hazardous business, this selective and
critical reading of the tradition. It is all too easy to filter out
whatever is antipathetic to our temperament, or too
challenging for our weakness. For example, I remember
reading some of Richard Meux Benson's books on religious
vocation, and being put off by the stress on self-abnegation.
I decided I didn't believe what he was teaching. It seemed to
me to be asking me to force my mind by means of my will.
Then, in an excess of zeal and humility, I said, "Okay, you
don't believe it. What exactly is it that you don't believe?
Outline the chapter, and then judge its consistency and its
truth." It was a helpful exercise, and left me with a soberer
estimate of self-abnegation. It did not, however, then or

ever, convince me that the "self" is bad. I was convinced, and have remained so, that the self, one's selfhood, is created by God in God's image, and is the supreme work of the divine creation. Years later, in Paul Tillich's *The Courage to Be*, I found support for my boldness.

There is a pervasive note of negative asceticism in much spiritual writing. Sometimes it is directed against the passions, the life of the flesh, desire and pleasure, and sometimes in later writers, against intellectual and spiritual development. This ascetic note begins, it seems to me, with the Greeks, and it has distorted our ideas of holiness and perfection. The exaltation of Mary as a virgin that took place in Christian tradition generally tended to distort or deny the fleshly reality of her marriage relationship with Joseph, a relationship which was central for them both, and to substitute an imagined "guardianship" for Joseph which has no substance for him, for Mary, or for Jesus. It is not mutual self-giving love that is at the center of the Holy Family of tradition, but a purity that must be acted out in the negative, in sexual abstinence. In this tradition, Mary the virgin is not allowed to be a real wife.

The same writers who give us so much of beauty and aspiration have also sown seeds of distortion in our self-understanding, which can be discerned in the difficulty so many of us today feel in really *accepting* forgiveness, in moving into and claiming the freedom, joy and power of renewal in grace, as well as in enjoying life in the flesh and in relationship.

In the period following New Testament times, from the second to the fifth century, the Christian message began to penetrate the civilized world of the West. The first Greek-speaking Christians, as we have noticed with the writers of the Greek New Testament, used the vocabulary and categories of a system of thought that dominated the eastern half of the Roman Empire. That system was Platonic;

Samuel Taylor Coleridge called the Platonic system "dear gorgeous nonsense," but it has influenced the imagination of the western world very deeply to our own day. Its legacy is both positive and negative. In the Hellenistic world-view there are other elements beside the Platonic, such as Stoicism, but Platonic dualism colored the whole.

Plato sometimes used myths to express his deepest, most subtle and most universal ideas. One famous myth is that of the charioteer and the banquet of the gods, found in the dialogue called the *Phaedrus*. In lively imagery it gives us a picture of the soul as Plato conceived it, in the form of a charioteer struggling with his two horses to get his chariot up to the heavens and the banquet of the gods. In this myth the charioteer, *nous* or intellect, is charged with the responsibility of guiding a pair of horses. One is noble, white and beautiful, and represents the positive aspect of human desire. The other horse is ugly, black, intractable, and lustful; it symbolizes what were for Plato the negative drives of lust, fear, and anger. The white horse thirsts for honor, tempered by modesty and restraint, and tends upwards toward the good of heavenly contemplation, the abode of the gods, while the black horse tends downwards toward the earth. The charioteer needs the energy of both horses to get him up toward the goal, but he alone can enter the highest heaven and contemplate eternal truth. The horses remain on a lower level and are fed, not at the banquet of the gods with its vision of true beauty, but with nectar and ambrosia.

Plato's teaching about the soul is imaged in this complex figure. The nature of the good life is a struggle by the intellect to subdue the passions; the true end of human life is the contemplation of the good, the true, and the beautiful. It is a dualistic pattern where intellect is associated with light, the divine, the heavens, over against the passions — ugliness, excess, darkness, and the earth. The virtues are masculine, active, dominant; the passions, feminine, passive, inferior. It is not a long step from this vision to a society organized and ordered by patriarchal values.

In Plato's time the feminine was considered inferior to the masculine and in need of governing, while women were considered unfit to govern. They were the property of their husbands, relegated to the domestic role. There were exceptions among women of wealth and leisure — as well as among the *heteirai*, who seem to have enjoyed intellectual converse with men and served as a superior kind of prostitute. Marriage was a social institution necessary for the procreation of children; the deepest part of a man's real life was found in his relationships outside the home.

Patriarchy tends to set great value upon the notion of mastery. Among the Greeks, mastery was expressed in terms of skill in the arts, in debate, and in asceticism. The idea of control of the lower by the higher parts of the soul was expressed in the value placed on the gymnasium and the open places in Greek cities used by men for conversation, debate, and intellectual exchange. In Hellenistic culture there is an essential asceticism associated with a negative attitude toward the passions and an emphasis upon simplicity, moderation, bodily training, and restraint.

Asceticism was never characteristic of Hebrew piety, with its holistic view of the human being, its acceptance of sexual pleasure in marriage, and its conviction that God did not want his people to be poor. Moderation was urged in the use of money and power, it was assumed that those with possessions and wealth would care for the poor, and purity in sexual relations was seen to reflect the holiness required by the holy God. Fasting, a universal ascetic practice, was communal and cultic, intended to impress and move the deity to mercy rather than to discipline the flesh. There is an ascetical strain in the Christian scriptures, but it concerns not the individual's struggle for perfection, but putting the kingdom of God first and taking up one's cross to follow Jesus. For Paul and the early church, the Christian way was a corporate one, not a lonely ascent to the heavens: "And they devoted themselves to the apostles' teaching and fellowship, to the breaking of bread and the prayers" (Acts 2:42).

What happened to the Christian gospel when it was expressed in terms of the Hellenistic culture of the first Christian centuries? In particular, what happened to the Judaeo-Christian teaching about the goodness of creation and the image of God in both male and female? What happened to Paul's vision of a community marked by humble, loving service and ministry, or to Christian marriage and the value placed upon feminine images and qualities? Finally, what images do we have from the Greeks of the meeting of opposites?

We shall look to one of the greatest theologians of the Hellenistic church, Gregory of Nyssa, for some answers to our questions about what happened to the Judaeo-Christian tradition concerning creation, marriage and community, and to Jesus' proclamation of the coming kingdom, when prostitutes and sinners will go in before the righteous.

Let me introduce Gregory briefly before we look in some detail at his teaching. He was born to an aristocratic family of Asia Minor, into the ruling class possessed of landed estates and accustomed to the best of everything, including education in the Greek schools. In some ways he was a not untypical younger son. He was not as lavishly equipped for life by his family as his older brother Basil was. He was not sent abroad to the great centers of Greek learning, but was educated at home by tutors and by Basil, as well as in the schools of rhetoric in his own country. He was pulled in two opposite directions: toward a worldly career and marriage, and toward the ideal of ascetical life.

He is both a representative theologian of the Christian East and a man capable of loving a woman, an author whose world view is influenced by a vision of the world which separated spirit from flesh, as we saw in the image of the charioteer. He was ambivalent about women and the feminine, torn between his own emotional and sexual experience and his understanding of Christian moral and spiritual teaching. Like Basil, he was greatly influenced by his older sister, Macrina, who had persuaded her mother Emmelia to embrace monastic life, and with her founded one of the first monastic communities of women. Gregory visited this community toward the end of Macrina's life, and in the treatise *The Soul and the Resurrection* he gives us an account of her teaching. This work is in the form of a dialogue between Gregory and Macrina. She is no "straw man," set up for demolishing by a more brilliant protagonist, but the teacher and guide of her younger brother. He was also present at her death, which he describes in *The Life of Macrina.*

Gregory's first treatise, *On Virginity*, was written at the urging of Basil. Its intent was to exalt the monastic, celibate state over marriage. Here we seem to see a contradiction within Gregory himself. He was either married to Theosobie, or he kept her as a concubine; in either case, he loved her. Upon her death Gregory Nazianzus, a close friend and fellow bishop, wrote a letter to Gregory of Nyssa consoling him in his bereavement, and calls her "our holy and blessed sister," which indicates a woman who shared his life. In her we seem to see the figure of a wife. Why is she called a sister? Were the two convinced that living together as brother and sister was the Christian solution to marriage, which Gregory's family could only regard as tragic, and which Basil and Macrina together had persuaded him to forsake?

Efforts to reconcile Christian and Greek ideas are plain in some of Gregory's writings. He says in the treatise *On Virginity*, "I am separated by an abyss from the glorious name of virgin, to which one may never again return once he has set his foot in the path of worldly life."[10] He speaks of the deceitful joys of marriage, joys which conceal the fear of death and change and loss. He speaks of the evils of childbearing and widowhood; virgins, he tells us, are spared these evils "because they live with a husband who is incorruptible." Evil, for Gregory, means something more like "misfortune," rather than moral evil. His comments here seem to reflect a reality he knew in his own life, and not merely commonplace rhetoric. He also says that passion begins in marriage and that in order to leave a good name to his family, a man must become involved in envy, rancor, hatred, and lust after material prosperity. On the other hand, Gregory writes, "Let no one think we condemn marriage. It has divine blessing." We are not to despise marriage, in other words, when it is lived with moderation and self-control. Hence the contradiction is not really resolved.

In his treatise *On the Soul and the Resurrection*, Gregory in a beautiful image compares us to a stalk of wheat: "In the spring of the resurrection [the earth] will reproduce this naked grain of our body in the form of an ear, tall, well-proportioned and erect, reaching to the heights of heaven, and, for blade and beard, resplendent in incorruption, and with all other God-like marks."[11] His teaching in *The Making of Man* says that the image of God in the human being resides in our spiritual nature alone, not in our bodily nature. For him the body is the image of the soul, the image of the image, and has its own subordinate goodness in relation to the soul. Reason and free will can direct the passions to a good end, but if reason drops the rein, the charioteer becomes entangled and the passions become fierce and destructive. It is God who rescues human beings from the trammels of passion, and his saving action is compared to relatives who drag corpses out of the rubble after an earthquake, to the work of a goldsmith refining metal by fire, and to the cleaning of a rope clogged by mud by dragging it through a hole. Hence the nature of the Christian's progress toward God is an ascent from earth to heaven, from domination by the passions to passionlessness.

We might suppose from this that the ascent to heaven is an experience of increasing purity and light until one arrives at the contemplation of the eternal, as in Plato. It is, therefore, a surprise to read in Gregory's *Life of Moses*, "leaving behind everything that is observed, not only what sense comprehends, but also what the intelligence thinks it

sees, it keeps on penetrating deeper, until by the
intelligence's yearning for understanding, it gains access to
the invisible and incomprehensible, and there it sees
God...This is the seeing that consists in not seeing...because
that which is sought transcends all knowledge, being
separated on all sides by incomprehensibility as by a kind of
darkness; therefore John the sublime who penetrated into the
luminous darkness says, 'No one has ever seen God,' thus
asserting that knowledge of the divine essence is
unattainable."[12]

This perception of the spiritual life differs from the one
Gregory inherited from Origen, for whom Christian progress
is an increasing illumination. Gregory's insight into the
mystery of the "luminous darkness" of our experience as we
approach God, and his understanding of the Christian life as
a progress which ever approaches but never reaches God
must spring from his own history. It forms the basis for a
contemplative spirituality, which teaches us to go beyond
thoughts, images and desires, and to reach out to God "in
naked intent," as the fourteenth-century author of *The Cloud
of Unknowing* puts it. This author, along with a mysterious
figure from the fifth century called "Dionysius the
Areopagite," John of the Cross in the sixteenth century, and
Thomas Merton in our own time, has given us the practical
and theological basis for such a spirituality. It is the
complementary approach to the more positive use of words
and images in prayer and meditation, found, for example, in
Ignatius of Loyola and Francis de Sales. In contemplative
prayer there is a movement of emptying, of letting go of
images, thoughts and desires, and in a more active kind of
meditation, images and thoughts and desires are used to
express our prayer. Probably both are integral to mature
Christian experience. Most of us make use at one time or
another of both ways, but tend to settle for one way as the
staple of our daily prayer. We may use words to explore
meaning and to express feeling, the imagination to help us
enter our own depths, and the will to bring our lives into

greater conformity with our vision. At other times we may use wordless or apophatic prayer. Apophatic prayer is lowly prayer, keeping us in stillness, waiting, emptiness. It does not speak of mastery or achievement, but of letting go and letting be. Its image of meeting is not a victory, though it may be a marriage or a banquet. Perhaps Gregory's own image is the best one, a luminous darkness which transcends all knowledge.

In *The Life of Macrina* we have a portrait of a Christian woman, Basil's elder sister who was responsible for his conversion. On the death of her fiancé, Macrina was determined to remain unmarried, to live "on her own." Henceforth she would not be dependent on parents or husband for her livelihood or her personal growth, but would take responsibility for her own life, a possibility open in those days only to women of affluence.

She founded a monastic community of men and women, and lived an ascetic life devoted to prayer, poverty and good works. Gregory visited her toward the end of her life, and said of her and of her community, "These women fall short of angelic and immaterial nature only insofar as they appeared in bodily form....Nor did she behave in any ignoble or womanish way....Nothing was left but the care of divine things, and the unceasing round of prayer and endless hymnody, coextensive with time itself, practiced by night and day." As Macrina was dying he wrote of her, "She was uplifted as she discoursed to us on the nature of the soul, and explained the reason of life in the flesh, and why human beings were made, and how we are mortal, and the origin of death, and the nature of the journey from death to life again....It did seem as if some angel had taken human form with a sort of incarnation. She had no kinship of likeness with this life of flesh."[13]

The resultant spirituality exalts the monastic life as an angelic life over marriage. It describes holiness as divinization, and as leaving the passions behind. Its attitude to the body and to the emotions is negative. Much of the spiritual literature of both eastern and western Christianity has been influenced by this position. Gregory praises Macrina for not grieving for the death of her mother, yet at the same time this entire treatise is full of passionate love and tender affection for this sister of his. In *The Soul and the Resurrection* she carries an equal part in the discussion. We do not know to what extent he puts his own words into her mouth, but the close relationship between the two suggests that he treated her as an equal, and perhaps as a superior; he calls her his teacher. In his treatise *On the Soul and the Resurrection* Gregory attributes to Macrina the comment that the passions are like "warts" growing out of the intellectual part of the soul. She involves herself in a contradiction when she maintains that we reflect the image of God only in our spiritual life, and at the same time tries to come to terms with the Christian doctrine of the resurrection of the body. It is a contradiction that points to the tension created when the Neo-Platonic system is confronted by the gospel of the Incarnation. Macrina went even further than Plato in her rejection of the passions, and Gregory approved.

Macrina's spirituality verges on what is called angelism, a heresy that denies the value of our fleshly life. In the Platonic image the desires are necessary for our journey to God, but Macrina would move beyond them to a purity which seems inhuman. It inhibited in her the normal experience of grief at the death of those she loved, especially her mother.

The basic image of the Christian life for the Greek Fathers and for Macrina is ascent. Many treatises in subsequent years were written on this theme. There are stairs, degrees, ladders, liftings up and strugglings up in many forms. We are exhorted to climb the ladder, the steps of humility, or the steps of divine love. Aspiring after the stars and the heavenly banquet is a powerful image which symbolizes an indispensible element in Christian spirituality: aspiration, engagement, risk and the love of excellence. Here is its positive legacy. It also has serious limitations and dangers, its negative legacy. Here are some of the dangers.

a) Ascent is limited to one movement alone, upwards. Yet we also need descent into ourselves; we must have confrontation with our own sources of woundedness and sin, where alone we find the way to repentance and transformation in Christ. The charioteer represents only half of the journey.

2) Another danger is that the journey can be abstracted or spiritualized to such a degree that it distances itself from the flesh and from relationships with other travelers. It can lead us to value heaven, purity and eternity, and devalue earth, passions, time and space, history and society. It can lead to a selfish fascination with our own interior experience, or to emotional impoverishment and unreality, even to denial and depression masked as mystical purgations and the "dark night of the soul."

3) The concept of the spiritual life as ascent and as progress can also lead us to concentrate on our interior journey without a corresponding return journey through the structures of our own relationships, the created earth and the social whole. Gregory of Nyssa provides us with a theological description of men and women as intermediate beings between material creation and the divine, and understands that the journey must include progress within our bodily and relational life, but Macrina's rejection of passions as "warts" will not do — even in Platonic terms — for the passions give the energy needed to achieve the upward journey.

4) Another limitation is the fact that ascent does not deal with "waylessness," a valid and valuable experience. Waylessness is the subject of many mystical writings, Christian and non-Christian, and is in contrast to the images which express movement and growth toward a goal, whether it be up or down or hidden. John of the Cross, a sixteenth-century Spanish mystic who was also a superb psychologist and poet, describes waylessness in terms of the "dark nights" which mark important transitions in the spiritual life. The passage from a less mature to a more mature faith or hope or love seems to require an emptying, a detachment from false goals and supports and images of self, and an entrance into desolation, dryness, a sense of being nowhere, in a fog with nothing to indicate direction. Everywhere one turns, it is the same — fog. But even in waylessness there is life, communication and growth. Purification takes a new form. It is more intimate and demands a deeper surrender. From bag ladies and drop-outs to Zen and Christian contemplatives, there ·is a real spirituality without clear waymarks.

On the other hand, there are realities in the image of the ladder, in the image of ascent and descent. A teacher is not as a pupil, a mother is not as a child, an artist is not as an apprentice. Not only confusion, but also tyranny, may result from overlooking or denying this. Humility, submission, obedience, are as proper to the human being as are domination, leadership and the imparting of instruction and wisdom. However, all of these are broadly human qualities, not definitions of sexual roles. Lowliness is not for women only, but for women and men. It is called out from both sexes as circumstances may require.

Descent is, therefore, a complementary and necessary theme. There are tunnels and caves, dark perils of the underworld to be mastered before one comes out into the place of purification and illumination, and the imparting of wisdom. Going down is a necessary preliminary to going up.

Jesus' life story has this pattern also. There is the forced march to be born in Bethlehem and the descent into Egypt when all the idols crashed as he passed, if we are to believe the legends; there is the modest, unheralded return to Nazareth, the going down of the "unoffending feet" into the waters of Baptism, and the dripping emergence from the water. There is Jesus' wilderness experience into the depths of temptation, with its sudden exaltation to the Temple pinnacle; there are the journeys taken by Jesus in his ministry, however they are mapped in the various gospel accounts, the entrance into Jerusalem on a donkey, the way of the cross, the descent into the tomb, the coming up again in the resurrection.

All these images express something about the spiritual journey, something about aspiration, hope and divinization. The baptismal rites of the Christian Church express both going down and coming up, dying to self and being born again. There is the dark experience of penitence. There is purification from evil, and the discovery of other kinds of riches. Mystery religions and primitive initiatory rites also require the dark journey, ordeal, terror, through which initiates must go. When we look at this pattern in general and think about it in relation to our own experiences, we may reflect that there is some meaning in ascent only when we also experience descent. We need both.

In our own day there are ascents through professional, academic and church life: grades, examinations, confirmations, promotions, and ordinations. Going through the processes of academic and professional training, climbing the ladder step by step, is exhilarating and enlarging. It is painful and laborious as well. It can cut us down to size in a healthy way, and present us with questions we have not heard and problems we have not faced. So also with psychotherapy, which can deepen our self-knowledge, release dammed-up energies, redirecting and freeing them for creativity, and deliver us from devouring childish rage, narcissism and illusion. The process also helps us grow in compassion for others. The cost is the discipline of patient and truthful engagement in the work of acquiring self-knowledge, an engagement which has a cost in humiliation and pain. Working through resentment, willfulness and illusion is both freeing and costly. We go down and then resurface in a different place — a wider place, where we can meet and interact with others more authentically.

When we turn to Gregory for models of meeting, of marriage between heaven and earth, between night and day, darkness and light, between the soul and the body, and between the sexes, we discover his notion of the human being as a means between two worlds, the divine and rational, and the irrational and the brutish, the purely spiritual and the purely material. This human being is the one to bring the whole creation to God, but we do not find in Gregory any clear concrete illustrations of how this is to work out, how spirit can use our passionate flesh to express the divine and the rational. When we turn to the gospels, we find that the goal of the Christian life is the kingdom and that marriage is the chief image of the kingdom. Yet we look in vain for such images in the Greek writers of the first five centuries. They took literally the description of the early church in the fourth chapter of Acts, and believed that the apostles were monks, leading a common life, possessing nothing of their own. They also believed that they remained unmarried as perfect followers of a celibate Jesus. Recognizing, however, that the Bible teaches that marriage is ordained and blessed by God, the Greeks arrived at a feeble compromise: marriage is a state of life inferior to a life of celibate chastity, permissible for Christians who cannot attain to the higher life of sexual abstinence. The banquet also became spiritualized as holy contemplation, removed from any physical embodiment. Even when Gregory tells us that "the bread which is consecrated by the Word of God is changed into the Body of God the Word," and speaks of God as "blending himself in the bodies of theirs to secure that, by this union to the immortal, man too may be a sharer in incorruption," he does not see the Eucharist as a corporate human reality, but rather almost as an escape from the body.[14]

The Christian life conceived of as an ascent, a normal metaphor for a patriarchal society and solitary achievement, is only half of the truth. It needs to be complemented by the vision of Paul of a community of mutual love and a shared ministry dedicated to bringing others to Christ. The gospel precepts about who is first in the kingdom of heaven qualify any ideal of ascetic perfection. The rejection of women as equal partners in ministry is another consequence of the patriarchal bias of Hellenistic culture, and was to remain dominant in the lives of Christians for centuries to come.

From Chariot to Flaming Heart

When we turn from east to west, from Athens to Rome,
and from Gregory of Nyssa to Augustine of Hippo, fourth-
century contemporaries and fellow bishops, we turn to the
culture which more than any other has marked the language
and social and political institutions of our western world.
Romanitas, "Romanness," describes the spirit which
combined the moral values and democratic institutions of the
early Roman empire with a vision of justice and peace for all
classes and nations under the aegis of Rome.

A curious incident a few years ago, during my only visit
to Italy, revealed to me my own share in this legacy from the
ancient world. I was wandering around the Roman forum
trying to imagine what it would have been like in its heyday.
I traced the foundation stones of the house of the Vestal
Virgins, and wondered about their privileges and their
renunciations. What did they do, for instance, in their free
time together? Did they play handball or other games? I
fancied Cicero being carried past me on a litter, busily
engaged in making notes on his wax tablet for a speech in
the Senate. I decided to find the Senate house and see it for
myself. I located the site and found the entrance intact, with
its great bronze doors ajar. Wild-looking, bony cats wreathed
around each other on the steps, and glared at me with
proprietary disdain and a certain menace. I spoke to them,
firmly and confidently. I said, *"This* is *mine."*

I meant more by this statement than a defiance of cats.
My own aspirations after world peace and justice came
together in the perspective of ancient history, and I
recognized my rootedness in the institutions and the spirit of

Rome. Those old classroom worthies — Caesar, Cicero and Virgil — came to life for me. Caesar's *clementia*, his preference for moderation and mercy over cruelty, and his statesmanship formed one strand of this spirit. Cicero formed another with his dogged defense of the rights of all classes of Romans, slaves only excepted, and his beautiful prose whose falling cadences Augustine echoed. Virgil focused *Romanitas* in his broad vision of the *pax Romana* over the whole civilized western world, his delicate and unprecedented awareness of human passions — even of women and children — and his sense of the "tears in things" gave it a dimension new to classicism. This is how Virgil speaks in book seven of the *Aeneid* of this vision and this promise:

> Yours will be the rulership of nations,
> remember, Roman, these will be your arts:
> to teach the ways of peace to those you conquer,
> to spare defeated peoples, tame the proud. (1134-7)

Augustine, born in the Roman province of Africa in the last days of the declining empire, inherited this spirit and this history. He was formed by his education in rhetoric in the values and vision of *Romanitas*, but he was not part of its power structure. His father was a minor official in the economically depressed class of the *curiales*, the wretched overburdened middle class. The ruling class was noted for its vices and cruelty, and the over-extended indefensible frontiers of the Empire were threatened by pressures from without, while within the decay of social and political life left it vulnerable and ready to fall.

When the young Augustine left Africa for Italy in pursuit of education in rhetoric, he met another spirit than *Romanitas*, a spirit which eventually captured him. It was the Christianity as it was preached and exemplified by Ambrose, Bishop of Milan. After Augustine's conversion his own long career as a Christian philosopher, theologian and administrator began. As Gregory in the east had wrestled with the questions raised for Christians confronted with a culture dominated by Hellenism, so Augustine in the west wrestled with the interaction between *Romanitas* and the gospel of Christ. The struggle wore one aspect when it involved Augustine's personal life of faith, worked out first in terms of a philosophy influenced by the dualism of the Neo-Platonists, and quite another when he became a bishop responsible for his diocese and embroiled in the theological controversies of his day.

The Latin Augustine wrote was the silver Latin of the Empire. It was not the golden Latin of the Roman Republic and its early Augustan period, the tongue of Caesar, Cicero, and Virgil, that I met and wrestled with in those dreary classrooms. If it is less "pure," in some sense, it is also richer, more flexible, and more apt for the expression of personal feeling. Perhaps Augustine himself made it so, as he used it to express depths of the human spirit and of his own heart that were never before articulated in Latin, or perhaps in any language. At the end of his life it was *caritas*, the love of God poured forth in his heart by the Holy Spirit, which fired him. Later tradition recognized this when it assigned to Augustine the symbol of the flaming heart.

In Gregory's younger contemporary, Augustine of Hippo, we can see how much the western church owes to the eastern tradition of spirituality, and we see some different ways of interpreting the doctrine of the divine image indwelling men and women, as well as some fresh images of meeting.

Augustine, like Paul, has a bad reputation in some quarters. Some of the reasons for this are his attitude toward women and marriage, his pessimism about the body, and a defensiveness in controversy which led him to one-sided and sometimes vitriolic condemnations of positions other than his own.

We need not look to Augustine for a consistent

theological system. He had an oceanic mind in which diverse currents met and interacted: Platonic and neo-Platonic, Judaeo-Christian, and his own developing spiritual awareness. This deeply introspective man was drawn out of himself by the burden and responsibility of his office as bishop. He moved through his life with a consistency of purpose — an unswerving effort to look within and find God, and to look without and find God there also. His positions changed, not in an erratic or irresponsible way, but honestly, often painfully, as his own personal horizons widened and his perceptions sharpened. He was not unaware of the shifts and contradictions in his thinking. He does not hesitate to admit that he has had to change his mind as the circumstances of his life and the exigencies of his episcopal responsibilities draw him to reconsider earlier certainties. In his old age he wrote a book called *Retractationes*, which we may translate as *Things I Have Been Wrong About.*

His contributions to theology are, of course, immense and far beyond my charting; for the purpose of this book we shall look at a few of his insights and images which have to do with our theme. The first is his understanding of the Christian life. In one of his earliest works Augustine gives us an image of the Christian life as an ascent to God, away from the earth and earthly things. He describes this ascent in philosophical terms, as a progressive spiritualization. In an early treatise he gives us a series of steps by which the soul rises toward God. The movement is from bodily life through the rational life to a state of inner repose, and thence to divinization and contemplation as immersion in God in forgetfulness of all else. The famous vision which he shared with his mother at Ostia, and which he relates in the ninth book of the *Confessions*, is described in neo-Platonic terms: "Raising up ourselves with a more glowing affection toward the 'self-same,' [we] did by degrees pass through all things bodily, even the very heaven...soaring higher yet by inward musing and discourse...we came to our own minds, and went beyond them" to that "wisdom by whom all things are made."[15] Plato's description of the ascent of the mortal charioteer through the lower heavens to the region beyond the skies of the heavenly banquet, and the contemplation of eternal truth, furnishes a close parallel and a background to the vision of Christian life as ascent, much as it did for the Greek Fathers.

In his *Commentary on the Psalms*, a much later work written toward the end of his life, Augustine describes a breakthrough in his own spiritual life when he applies to himself and to the church the consequences of his doctrine of grace. In commenting on Psalm 42 (41 in his Latin version) he realizes that the soul cannot attain to God by seeking him either in created things or in one's own self. The soul can find God only if God comes to the soul. And God does come down to us, in the incarnation of Jesus and in the church, and there we meet him. "For he who possesses, beyond the highest heavens, an invisible mansion, has also a tent on earth. His tent is his church, still on pilgrimage."[16] Here the emphasis in Augustine differs from that of the Greek Fathers. He shifts the ground of our hope from ascetic effort, mastery of the passions, to the free gift of grace, and he amplifies the description of the work of God in us by adding to deification an emphasis upon God's initiative.

Grace, for Augustine, and for the whole western church since his day, is above all God's sovereign freedom and loving will to save us. It transforms our will, energizes our love, enables us to obey the gospel precepts and to do good. Without it we can do no good thing. It is also a mystery, and Augustine recognizes this when he calls it so and adds that he prefers ignorance to rashness in defining it.

With his "*ecclesia peregrina*," the church on pilgrimage, he gives us a new image. The ascent motif is here applied not to the soul in solitude, but to the whole body of the faithful, God's people, and here amidst his brothers and sisters on earth, Augustine must find the way that leads to his goal. This, his final understanding of the Christian life, is a more humble one than his earlier one. It begins with our entrance

into the church at baptism. We are fed there with others at
the common meal of the Eucharist and by Christian doctrine,
and share a common journey. Through the Christian
community on earth lies the way to God's eternal dwelling.
The church itself, the Body of Christ, is on pilgrimage.
Augustine applied this image to the great collectivities of his
day — to the church and to the city. Rome and *Romanitas*
were for him corporately fallen, and not merely a collection
of fallen individuals. The church was corporately moving
toward God; Augustine, one of its bishops, moved with it and
by its energy, the energy of love. He saw the sacraments,
baptism and the Eucharist, in this light. Finally, his doctrine
of grace clearly implied that the journey of each individual
soul depended on its participation in the grace given to the
church. The Fourth Gospel gives us, as the words of Jesus,
this arresting claim: "I am the way." Augustine saw that
unless the "way" came down to us, neither he nor anyone
else would reach the goal. The embodied way is further
developed in later writers, especially in Dante and in Dante's
commentators.

Augustine has thus fused two images of the Christian
life, one from the Acts of the Apostles — Christian life as
community — and one from the Greek image of ascent,
symbolized by the charioteer and his horses.

We turn now to look at some of Augustine's comments on
the keys of the kingdom. First, he understands these keys to
have been given by Christ to Peter and hence to the church,
and to stand as an image of authority. He writes, "Unhappy
are those who do not believe that the keys of the kingdom of
heaven have been given to the church — they have lost them
from their grasp."[17] It is perhaps surprising that Augustine
emphasizes the merciful and liberating power of the keys,
rather than their bestowal of authority to bind, to lock up, to
punish. He is not exactly clear about this, and furthermore
what he says in his early writings is not always echoed in
later ones after he became a bishop and was forced to
struggle with teachers and other bishops who opposed him.

Augustine does speak of the keys as symbols of patience, and not only as symbols of power. Addressing God, he says, "The only power the keys of the kingdom have in your church is that no one must be despaired of so long as he lives on this earth, because of your patience."[18] In *The City of God*, written at the end of his life, Augustine has this to say about earthly power and authority: "It is characteristic of the earthly city to pray that God may reign victoriously by conquest; not by loving persuasion, but by lust of domination."[19] Here again he contrasts victory with persuasion, and recognizes the danger inherent in the love of power. It seems that Augustine did not lose sight of Jesus' words about lordship: "Let the greatest among you become as the youngest, and the leader as one who serves" (Lk. 22:26). Elsewhere Augustine writes, "Love of mastery disturbs and wears down the human race" (4.14). As for Augustine himself, his biographer Possidius in describing his life among the monastic clergy of the diocese, says that Augustine wore no ring and carried no key. I like to imagine Augustine asking the cellarer of his community for what he needed.

Dominion and mastery, we have seen, exist in us as a reflection of God's sovereignty over creation. This idea was reinterpreted by Jesus in his radical teaching that leaders are servants. Augustine the philosopher met Augustine the Christian at the end of his life, and gave us the beginning of a reinterpretation of authority and a glimpse into some new ways of perceiving and acting out the authority bestowed on us with the imprint of the divine image at creation. It is an image of authority as ministry, with the keys of the kingdom as humble, domestic instruments of stewardship.

Another important element in Augustine's legacy to us is his doctrine of the Trinity, one which is crucial for the theology of our creation in God's image. We have seen that the Greek Fathers located the image of God in our spiritual nature; Augustine located it in the dynamism of the Holy Trinity: "We recognize in ourselves the image of God, that is, of the Supreme Trinity."[20] He learned the way to an immanent Trinity from the economic Trinity of the Greek Fathers, and developed the theme in his treatise, *On the Trinity*. He looked within himself and seemed to recognize a threefoldedness there, describing this inner triad in various ways — as memory, understanding, and will, and as mind, self-knowledge, and love. Augustine was the first theologian to find a reflection of the Trinity within the experience of an individual person. His triads were used in later tradition to outline a structure for ordered meditation on the Bible in the Ignatian exercises. In praying about a biblical passage, we recall the scene, dwelling upon its sensory details, we think about what it means, in itself and for us individually, and we react to it with our affections and our wills. Prayer is then seen as an activity which is an image of God, mirroring the energies of love in the inner life of the Godhead. In this significant departure from the earlier Greek anthropology, which located the image (defined as the image of the Father, or of the Son) in the higher as opposed to the lower part of the soul, Augustine laid the groundwork for a new, more active, spirituality.

G. L. Prestige points out that Augustine, in *On the Trinity*, paves the way "to the conception of the mutual interpenetration of the three Persons."[21] If the whole Trinity is imaged in each of us, then each of us is fully human. If the threefold energy of love in the Trinity can be described in terms of "mutual interpenetration," the way is prepared for a social interpretation of the Trinity, and to an intercommunion of equal persons, women and men, in human sociality as a reflection of the life of God. Augustine himself failed to see the implications for both genders of this teaching. Instead he taught that women share the image of God only through the man, because the body of woman is weak and prone to sin. He quotes Paul in support of this position, in I Corinthians 11:2-12, where the man is said to be the "head" of the woman, and "the image and glory of God, but woman is the glory of man." However, we have noted that this passage is out of harmony with other Pauline writing, and is by some considered to be an interpolation by a later hand. Whether or not it was written by Paul, it is best understood as a commentary on the Genesis account of the creation of woman from the body of man, who is not her "head" in the hierarchical sense, but, as in Genesis, the source of her body. Her spirit is from God.

Augustine also contained the tradition which held that the natural inferiority of woman was reflected in her weaker body and her tendency to sin. Among Latin theologians, Thomas Aquinas was later to teach the God-ordained inferiority of women to men. For Augustine, on this question a Platonist, the inferiority of women had to do with bodily differences and did not reflect, as it did for Aquinas, an inferiority of the soul. Still later Luther held that the woman was equal to the man in the original creation, but her inferiority and subjection to the male arose as a punishment for sin.

Augustine's attitude to women and to the feminine has been studied and been exhaustively discussed in current literature from the point of view of psycho-biography. His early life, as he reports it in the *Confessions*, has also been examined in the light of various schools of psychological analysis. Augustine's relationship to his mistress seemed to be one that carried little real commitment to the woman, whom he deserted upon his conversion to Christianity and whom he does not even name. His suffering over this parting appears to arise more from self-pity and frustrated lust than from any concern for her as a person, much less as a woman who intimately shared his life.

His view of sexuality is negative, guilty, and shame-ridden. For Augustine the essence of the fall of the first human couple was the loss of rational control over the body, particularly over the phallus. To think that lust can be tamed is a delusion. So for Augustine the sex act, which is not under the control of the rational mind and will, but seems to take place on its own, is sinful and transmits original sin to every child that is born of the flesh.

His interpretation of the creation story in Genesis involves the conclusion that Eve was taken from Adam's side because she was given to him for the purpose of helping him. The feminine body is obviously weaker and inferior, half-baked as it were, compared to the masculine. Only through man can woman share in the image of God in her body. Nor does Augustine see a relationship between the Holy Trinity and marriage as a meeting of woman and man together, reflecting the image of God in mutual love. Marriage, he says, is for procreation and not for pleasure, and childbearing is the only thing a woman can do better than a man. A man might love his wife as he loves his enemies, Augustine said. Later in his life he modified this statement, and conceded that conjugal embraces are not only lawful, but delightful. He does not move beyond this. Of course, he has no personal experience of Christian marriage. It is not Augustine's immanent Trinity, wholly within himself, which gives us a model for Christian marriage.

Finally, we look at his teaching about love and the different kinds of love: "Who can map out the various forces at play in our soul? Man is a great depth, O Lord," he asks in his *Confessions*. On the eve of his baptism Augustine wrote, "I long to know God and my own soul." The love of friendship, especially between men, was highly esteemed and discussed at length in schools of philosophy. Friendship was of supreme importance to Augustine. His early life, and his examination of that life in the *Confessions*, shows us a man driven by love — by many loves. All his life he loved contemplation, and he loved his friends. In answer to the question, "Will the purest beauty of Wisdom reveal itself to you unless you burn for it alone?", he replied, "I do love Wisdom alone, and for its own sake. And it is on account of Wisdom that I want to have or care about other things, such as life, tranquillity and my friends."[22] It was his friends, his fellow monks and bishops, who remained with him to the end rather than tranquillity. He lived and died in a celibate, contemplative community, burdened by the episcopal office in a time of turmoil.

Augustine dwelt at length, even obsessively, on the negative side of love, with love as desire, as sinfully inordinate, which is what he means by concupiscence.

His vision of "ordered loves" he developed later in his life. Rufinus had translated The Song of Songs 2:4 as "*ordinate in me caritate*," "set love in order within me." Augustine uses this in *The City of God*: "Bodily loveliness, though made by God, is nevertheless a temporal, carnal and lowly good. It is wrongfully loved if it is valued above God the eternal, inward and lasting good. Just as the covetous man subordinates justice to his love of money, through no fault of the money but in himself, so it is with all things. In themselves they are all good, and they can all be loved well or badly. They are loved well when the right order is kept in loving, badly when it is upset" (15.22). For all his severity about excessive desire, especially fleshly desire, Augustine's teaching about love was founded upon the positive commandment at the heart of Christian teaching, the commandment to love God and to love our neighbors as we love ourselves. He saw that this involves a right love of self. We must learn the right way of this loving, he said, and this includes a wise love and care for our bodies, and the bodies of our neighbors as well as their souls.

Augustine's spiritual legacy is immensely complex, with positive and negative contributions that are alive and well in the Christian community today. His convictions about the divine image in us have limited our understanding of our own nature to the image of the male, but they have offered us hope for a renewed human collective in the divine image. Augustine's teachings have also darkened women's self-image by insisting that they have inherited a nature damaged from its inception by the taint of sexuality, the lust of the flesh. Carnality, fleshliness, entails a reversal of true order, he says; passions should be controlled by a will and intellect, as Plato had taught. The divine image was distorted by the Fall and a stigma attached to sexual union, linking it fatefully with fear, anxiety, and shame, involving us all in original sin.

The hopeful, liberating side of Augustine's doctrine of the image of God in us emerges when we look at his doctrine of a Trinity within each of us. The Trinity in Greek thought had been described in terms of persons and their social relationships. Augustine looked within himself and saw in his own threefoldedness of memory, reason and will, that the Trinity is also within. Our inner activity, when it is brought into harmony with divine grace, includes the experience of opening our hearts to God. Receiving forgiveness and a fresh infusion of the energy of love, as well as the act of loving others, is not only a gift of God but a reflection or model of God's own life. It is the pattern of our inner life. His "pilgrim church" gives us a dynamic model for our spirituality, and at the end of his life, in *The City of God*, he points us toward still another dimension of the doctrine of the divine image when he underlines the unity and solidarity of the human race. "Nothing is so discordant when it deteriorates, nor so social in its true nature, than the human race" (12:129). Augustine did not apply this pattern to the collectivities of his day. It lies to hand for our own day when distorted social images threaten the peace and freedom and well-being of the human race on such a broad front.

If Augustine is the "doctor of grace," he is also a doctor of love and humility. Torn though he was by conflicting loves, he found words to express his longing for inner harmony and his faith in the priority of love. "Set love in order within me," he prays. Humility is for Augustine not merely one virtue among others, but the necessary corollary of his teaching about our need for Christ. Our dependence on God, our emptiness and need before him, our deep thirst for his love, the receptivity of our God-given human nature — all these form our living response to sovereign grace.

In spite of his intransigence toward those teachers who disagreed with him, and a certain defensive narrow-mindedness in controversy, Augustine the bishop knew humility in his personal life. He did not absolutize his episcopal powers. The keys of the kingdom given to the church and placed in his care were not so much for the locking up of sinners as for the unlocking of mercy. Augustine was not unmindful of how Jesus reinterpreted the power and dominion given by God to the first human pair, remembering that the one who would be first must be last and the servant of all.

A new way of understanding how we reflect the image of God began to emerge with Augustine. Toward the end of his life he perceived that the Trinity is found in the threefoldedness of human spirit, a new insight that sprang not from analysis and logical reasoning, but from his experience. As far as I know, Augustine never developed this idea in relation to marriage, nor did he see any way in which the feminine could mirror the divine being. His negative estimate of the flesh, its feelings and drives, kept him from exploring the possibility of divine revelation in the love between the sexes. It was for later ages to explore the implications of the trinitarian formula for sexuality.

The Image in Dante

I sat alone on the floor in the "red library" of my
secondary school, looking for something to read. I pulled
down a heavy leather-bound volume which turned out to be
Dante's *Inferno*, with illustrations by Gustave Doré. I can
still see some of those engravings in my mind's eye: a pope
upside down in a flaming pit; the lovers whirled forever in a
roaring circle of wind, never united and never separated; the
dark wood with its three beasts; the poet himself with Virgil
beside him, looking with such dread into the abyss of
darkness and pain. I sampled the poem itself. I remember
still the fate of the slothful, immersed in mud, because "in
the sweet air they were sad;" and the ever-tightening circles
of the tormented and damned, until with Dante and Virgil I
came to the frozen bottom of the pit where the great traitors
lay: Brutus and Cassius, Judas, and Satan himself. It was
terrifying and fascinating.

I can also recall my rejection of the whole thing. Where
was this hell? Nowhere. Nothing in reason, decency, or
Scripture warranted that infernal geography. To my teenaged
intellect the whole notion of hell was a repulsive figment of
the unenlightened medieval mind. Another book of pictures,
probably Foxe's Book of Martyrs, resonated in my memory
with those of Doré's Dante. I wanted none of it, none of a
God who created such a place or permitted it to exist.

Later, when I was in college, I read the poem through
along with the *Paradiso*. Somehow I skipped the second
book, the *Purgatorio*, entirely, and understood only a little of
the first and third books. Later still I discovered William
Blake's illustrations for the *Paradiso*. I had no more

understanding of Blake's philosophy and cosmography than of Dante's own, but I loved his tender color, the strong sure lines with which he rendered bodily loveliness.

The *Purgatorio* was the last to become real to me, and not so much through illustrations as through Dorothy Sayers' translation and Daniel Berrigan's commentary, *The Discipline of the Mountain: Dante's Purgatorio in a Nuclear World.*

When a few years ago I happened to read a contemporary interpretation of *The Divine Comedy*, *Dark Wood to White Rose*, by Helen Luke, I was determined to read the whole poem through, taking the books in order. I went unflinchingly down through the circles and trenches of hell, through every one in the stifling murky atmosphere, to the bottom of the pit. I crawled along the hairy legs of Satan, was turned upside down in the process to emerge at last, right side up, to see the stars again and breathe a different air. I climbed the ledges of the Mount of Discipline, through the fiery cleansing ring of molten glass at the top, to the earthly Paradise where Beatrice appears. Up once more I went, through the heavenly spheres to the final vision of the Rose and the Trinity with a human face, the face of Christ.

For the first time I realized that Dante's journey was my journey. I saw that the "geography of hell" I had rejected was the image of my own inner journey, my descent into sin and my immersion in sinfulness. The ledges of purgation were mine, and at last I too caught a tiny glimpse of the white rose, the golden bees of the heavenly choir, and the "love that moved the sun and the other stars."

Dante was a poet first and foremost; then he was a theologian, philosopher, politician, husband and father and friend and lover. The images he used, like those of the great Platonic myths, have haunted the imagination of the western world through the centuries ever since. How do we see these images now, in the perspective of Christian anthropology, today? How do they relate to the biblical themes of the image of God reflected in the first human couple and in every man and woman? To do this, we need to understand Dante's own method of interpretation.

The exegesis of literature, and in particular of Scripture, in medieval times was based upon a fourfold division of levels of meaning: the literal, the allegorical, the moral, and the anagogical or mystical. This represents an elaboration of the earlier patristic exegesis which used the literal or historical level and the spiritual level in dealing with the Bible. By Dante's time the spiritual level was divided into three. Dante himself describes the fourfold method he used in a letter to his friend and patron, Can Grande della Scala. A Latin tag explains each level:

> *Littera gesta docet,*
> *quid credas allegoria,*
> *Moralis quid agas,*
> *quo tendas anagogia.*

> The literal meaning is what happened,
> the allegorical what we must believe,
> The moral meaning tells us what to do,
> the anagogical whither we go.

So the first level of meaning in Dante is the story. The allegorical meaning of the story reflects the faith of the church. The moral meaning illuminates duty, sin, virtue and judgment. The anagogical or mystical deals with spiritual experience, vision and union with God.

My own approach to *The Divine Comedy* was through the *Purgatorio*. It was the first of the three books which engaged me fully. It challenged and judged and shamed me in the concrete reality of the memories it stirred in me, memories of my own past deeds and desperations. It showed me how to deal with the *Inferno*. The images of suffering in each book are almost equally ugly and dreadful. It is the attitude of the sufferers which differs so markedly, a change which Dante suggests by the contrast he draws between the oppressive atmosphere of hell and the freshness of the air at the base of the Mount of Purgation. In the *Inferno* the souls of the damned are filled with hatred and malice. They rail against their fate, against God and against each other. They suffer with rage. The souls in the *Purgatorio* accept their punishments, which are sometimes as grotesque as those of hell, with gentleness and humility, with awareness of and compassion for one another. The only way I can face the distorted images of humanity which abound in every life, in my life, in the life of the festering cities and lonely places in our world, is to see them as provisional, as pictures of what might be if we choose to remain as we are. The images can also serve as antechambers of preparation and purgation, signs of hope, of the possibility of change, and of a city to be revealed.

The image of a distorted creation first appears in Genesis where thorns and briars disfigure the earth, and painful toil and childbearing make heavy and burdensome the daily experience and relationships of men and women. The distortion of the image of God in our primal parents resulted in the severing of the bonds of mutuality between the sexes and the imposition of one will over against the other. Likewise, the images of the poem are derived from the poet's experience and inspiration. They point toward another kind of image which does not arise from experience, but is imprinted upon each of us by God at our creation. It is an image which reflects its divine maker, which was supremely revealed in Jesus Christ, and will be fully revealed at the general resurrection, when the distortions shall be healed.

In the thirteenth century a voice was lifted up from a milieu very different from the world of monastic spirituality which formed Gregory of Nyssa and Augustine of Hippo. Dante Alighieri was neither monk nor cleric, but a married layman. As a theologian he was trained in the scholastic theology of Thomas Aquinas, and influenced also by

Augustine and the Franciscans. He was a humanist and a
philosopher, with a love for the ancient world and a keen
awareness of his Roman inheritance, a Florentine, a politician
and a man of affairs, and a bitter critic of the corruptions of
the church and of the popes. Most of all he was a poet.
Thomas Merton speaks of what we may expect from poets —
new fruits of hope for the world. In a message read to a
meeting of Latin American and North American poets in
1964 he said: "Let us obey life, and the Spirit of Life that
calls us to be poets, and we shall harvest many new fruits for
which the world hungers — fruits of hope that have never
been seen before. With these fruits we shall calm the
resentments and the rage of man."[23]

In the *Vita Nuova*, Dante tells us of an intense spiritual
experience in his childhood which dominated his imagination
and oriented his journey for the rest of his life. He was
nearly nine when his father took him to a May Day party at
the house of Folco Portinari, a wealthy Florentine citizen,
and here he met his host's little daughter, a child about a
year younger than himself. "She was dressed in a very noble
color, a rich and subdued red, girded and adorned in a
manner becoming to her very tender age." Dante declared
"most truly that at every moment his heart trembled and
said, 'Behold, a god, stronger than I, has come to rule over
me,' and that his soul and intellect began to marvel, and said,
'Now is your bliss made manifest,' and that his senses
lamenting replied, 'Alas, how often henceforth shall we be
troubled.'" So Dante told the story twenty years later, and
the poetic manner of his telling need not make us doubt the
essential truth of the story.[24]

He never forgot the child's name nor allowed the world
to forget it. That name is Beatrice, which means
"blessedness."

Beatrice was for Dante "a mirror in which, at the height
of his powers and to the end of his days, he beheld all
heaven and earth reflected."[25] His encounter with her was
not the beginning of a romance leading to marriage. The

medieval view of marriage and sexual love was different from ours. Marriage was a family affair, entered into for dynastic or economic reasons and as such it was blessed by the church. It had little or nothing to do with romantic love as we think of it. On the other hand, the tradition of lyric verse in Latin and in the vernacular, which Dante inherited, expressed "the complexity and psychology of human sexual love...and the special quality and evolutionary possibilities of the nature of womankind which had been debased in the secular society and was ignored by the ecclesiastical tradition."[26] The debasing and the ignoring are linked consequences of the failure of Christian theology and spirituality to remember and live out the truth of the statement in Genesis that the earth creature, male and female together, is in the image of God, who said, "Be fruitful and multiply."

In the culture of Dante's day sexual love could lead to adultery, which was sin in the eyes of the church, or it could be transmuted into Platonic love. "The process would seem to involve a transformation of sexual energy through which the love of the lady's exterior form would dissolve into the love of the miraculous revelation of her soul, and, by implication, to a universal love of the maker of her soul."[27] Such an experience could hardly lead to marriage, and both Dante and Beatrice married other people. Beatrice died in 1290, and it seemed to Dante that all Florence was widowed by her death, and his own life darkened. Her image remained with him to the end.

Perhaps the most comprehensive thing one might say concerning Beatrice is that for Dante she embodied his experience of life. It was her wisdom, her humility and her charity that were "stamped on him as a fundamental experience." Dante's special and unique genius lay in his ability to see in one person, this beautiful woman who never loses her concrete historical reality, the affirmation of images: the city, the church, and Christ himself. As Charles Williams points out, Beatrice was the means by which Dante's

experience and his vision were enlarged and complemented
by hers. As she became his teacher and guide, he became
her handmaid: "His own soul is to be the feminine, the God-
bearer, the Mother of Love....In this sense there is already
proposed the mortal maternity of God which is fully exposed
in the conclusion of the *Paradiso*." Beatrice heightens his
masculinity. In answer to her challenge, "the thing that
moves his mind is *valore* — worth, value, valor. Her beauty
springs fierce before him and he answers by declaring the
particular virtue of a man."[28]

Some of the insights that were put into a new light by
Dante and his poem have a special bearing upon our theme.
They include the role of a woman, Beatrice, in fostering his
spiritual progress, the place and meaning of descent in the
spiritual life, his and ours, and the need for humility in those
who rule as well as in those who are ruled.

The figure of Beatrice, a historical flesh-and-blood
young woman, neither an ideal nor an allegory, is crucial in
the poem and in Dante's whole life. If earlier tradition, with
some exceptions like Macrina, had largely left women in an
inferior and dependent position, and denied them a voice in
the church as well as the functions of teaching and
interpreting Scripture, preaching and guiding men, Beatrice
does all of these things. Through her ministry Dante comes
to himself, to his own autonomy. She guides and he follows;
she explains and rebukes and he accepts; she invites, shames
and encourages, and he takes heart and ventures. Together
they mount toward the final goal of the journey.

Descent as a prelude to ascent is also important for our
understanding of Dante's journey and our own. We have
seen how Augustine, through his own growing experience of
life in the Christian community at Hippo modified his earlier
Platonic image of the Christian life from a solitary ascent to
a common journey. Dante modifies ascent by associating it
with its opposite and complement, with descent. In the
lowest pit of hell, awareness of the deepest roots of evil

within becomes awareness of a new direction and the energy which leads up and out.

Humility has often been seen as feminine, or as especially suitable for women, while aspiration and victorious adventuring are assigned to men. In Dante, humility is a counterpoise for both sexes, to aspiration, and a curb to ambition and domination. He chooses for two of his examples of these virtues a King and an Emperor, whose power was tempered by lowliness and self-forgetfulness. His interpretation also of the two keys, one gold and one silver, symbols of papal power, has the same thrust: for Christians, power must be exercised with compassion and humility after Christ's example. Dante's own gracious submission to his guides throughout the poem illustrates the same point.

To be made in the image of God, male and female, and given dominion over creation, is understood in Dante's poem as involving an exchange between sexual opposites and the virtues associated with each sex, and the interpretation of the divine command to "have dominion" over the other orders as requiring the tempering of that power by the gentleness and lowliness of humility.

Dante is concerned that women should be able to read his poem. The reason he gave for writing it in the vernacular, in Italian rather than Latin, was so that women might read it. The Italian tongue was one "in which even women can exchange ideas," as he remarked. In saying this, he meant no disrespect for women, but merely wanted every intelligent person in Italy to read it.

The Divine Comedy is written in three books, the *Inferno*, *Purgatorio*, and *Paradiso*. It is Dante's greatest poem, written at the end of his life, long after the death of Beatrice, and the work that has the most to say to us about spirituality. It was written entirely, or almost entirely, after his exile from Florence in 1302. It was the vision of the "holy and glorious flesh" as he beheld it in Beatrice which opened for Dante a spirituality centered not, as with the Greek Fathers, upon a progressive purification from the flesh and its passions, but precisely on its opposite. Dante implicitly rejected the monastic tradition of spirituality, which was the "way of the rejection of images," and offered instead a spirituality of the "affirmation of images," a spirituality which arose for him from a vision of Eros, and led up to a vision of God in highest heaven. Purification in *The Divine Comedy* is a progressive acceptance, a centering into, the life of the flesh and of the community. In a costly and relentless progression, desire is purified but not eliminated or weakened.

The whole of the poem is dominated by the motif of journey. It is never a journey alone, however. Dante has companions: first Virgil, then Beatrice, and finally Bernard. He learns about himself from his guides, from these others whose experiences he observes. We learn from this that a journey through hell, purgatory and heaven is also a journey in a vision, and the vision is a gift from God through the intervention of Beatrice, whose goodness and beauty, wisdom and charity, were, for him, an opening into an understanding of what his own life could be.

The three stages into which the journey is divided correspond in some ways to the three stages of purgation, illumination and union. While the *Inferno* is not purgative in a strict theological sense, because nothing changes there, a good deal changes in the reader. None of us can go down with Dante in imagination through the circles of ever-deepening horror and look upon those images of what sin is, and fail to recognize our own image, distorted by the perversion of love and of loves. *Purgatorio* is the place of purification and illumination where the image is progressively restored, while *Paradiso* is the place where the image of the Trinity becomes one with the human face of Christ.

Beatrice is central to this journey. Dante ultimately comes to say of her: "If Christ is holy Wisdom, then Christ is the woman I love, in whom holy Wisdom is manifest to me." Henceforth, the flesh of a woman is holy and glorious, capable of the revelation of a supreme God. She is the actual illuminating image of his whole life, and she is the image of Christ for him. But before Beatrice can be this, transformation has to take place in Dante himself. His bitter anger and despair, his loathing of so much in his experience, especially the corruptions of the church and of the state — as well as the failures of love in his personal life, about which he tells us himself and to which his experience in the last cornice of purgatory seems to point — must be purged and its energy transmuted. The whole journey through hell and purgatory symbolizes this transformation and the necessity of coming face to face with the ugliness of sin and evil.

At the beginning of the *Inferno*, which takes place on Good Friday, Dante awakes to find himself in a dark wood "where the right road was wholly lost and gone." After an encounter with the three beasts — leopard, lion and wolf, images of the sins of lust, pride, and avarice — he meets the shade of Virgil, the first of his guides, who tells him how Beatrice had gone to him in the underworld and sent him to Dante's rescue. Rescue, however, does not begin as a way out, or a way up. It begins with a way down. Virgil, who accompanies Dante as guide and mentor and sometimes nurse, warns him of what lies ahead:

> ...an eternal place and terrible
>
> Where thou shalt hear despairing cries, and see
> Long-parted souls that in their torments dire
> Howl for the second death perpetually. (1:114-7)

Dante tries to excuse himself from the journey, but Virgil coaxes and shames him through those ominous gates with their warning, "Abandon hope, all you who enter."

Dante's *Inferno* is not a place, but a vision of *what might be*. We see in relentless and concrete detail what sin is — our sin. We are confronted with the necessity of keeping on, going down into the darkest center of our sinfulness, recognizing step-by-step our own kinship with the condemned. We are spared nothing on this journey. We see what our own lust, indulgence, dishonesty, hatred and treachery really look like. There is no way out from the contemplation of our ultimate baseness, our betrayal of God. We must go through to the very bottom, the frozen center of hell where the traitors are, Brutus and Cassius along with Judas. Only by crawling down the hairy legs of Satan himself do we find the upside-down passageway out. What a relief it is, when, having gone through *Inferno*, skipping nothing, we emerge from it with Dante and Virgil and with them rejoice to breathe a different air and "to look once more upon the stars."

Purgatory is only the beginning of a new stage. More than anything else in all of the literature of spirituality, this poem conveys the sense of repentance as gift and as acceptance. The atmosphere of purgatory is totally different from that of hell. Remorse, anger and hatred are gone and forgotten. Because they accept their suffering in humility, the sinners here are open to its cleansing and renewing power. There is a freshness, a stillness and a mutuality in purgatory. Even in the circle of fire, where lust is purged, the sinners being cleansed salute each other, touch and kiss each other lightly. In hell, the sinners are totally immersed in gloom and hatred of themselves and of each other. Their conversations with Dante reveal attitudes of envy and hostility toward others in the same place. Those in purgatory have accepted responsibility for their sins, and endure their purgation with hope and in solidarity with one another. *Community*, wholly lost in hell, is here already restored.

The plan of the *Purgatorio* to some extent reverses the plan of the *Inferno*. Dante sees the experience of purification as a journey, this time a journey up a mountain. But here the sufferers *move*. From time to time some soul, having paid the penalty of sin, is released and rises to the earthly paradise while the whole mountain sings for joy.

What Dante experiences is passive. He looks at, is impressed by, and reacts to first the suffering, then the purification, and finally the joy of others. At the very end of the journey, however, at the climax of the poem, the vision becomes uniquely his own:

> For now my sight, clear and yet clearer grown,
> Pierced through the ray of that exalted light,
> Wherein, as in itself, the truth is known.
> *(Par.* 33:52-4)

Dante sees within the threefold spheres of the Trinity a human face, "limned with our image" (131). He becomes one with that which he has sought in his long and arduous journey.

What Dante also gives to us is a fresh way of looking at the great Christian virtue of humility, not as an ascetical or monastic achievement, but as the virtue of those who have dominion and power over others in church and state. Our ancestors in the faith were impressed by the divine command in Genesis 1:26-28, to have dominion over the earth and its creatures, to subdue them. The verbs are strong. They suggest trampling over rough ground, beating down savagery and ordering disorder. When this commandment is taken by itself — out of relationship to its context of our creation in the divine image, of which it is the consequence — it leads to pride and oppression. When we remember that we bear the image of God who is both righteous and compassionate, we see that we are to exercise power lovingly, mercifully, and humbly. Dante suggests this in his interpretation of the two keys in the ninth canto of the *Purgatorio*, keys which traditionally represented the power of the church derived from Peter.

The entrance to Purgatory is through Peter's Gate, which is approached by the three steps of penitence: confession, contrition, and satisfaction. As each soul passes through it receives the marks of the seven sins upon its forehead, marks that are erased one by one as the soul progresses up the mountain of discipline and the seven cornices of Purgatory with their cleansing punishments. On each of these cornices, where the sins of pride, envy, anger, acedia (spiritual sloth), covetousness, gluttony, and lust are purged, there are representations of examples of each of the opposite virtues. Drawn from tradition and Scripture, these pictures are intended to move the penitents to emulation, while another set reproduced the bad end of those who have not repented of these sins.

At the entrance to Purgatory, as Dante and Virgil approach its gate, they find their way barred by an angel seated at the top of the three steps that reflect the medieval understanding of the sacrament of penance. The first is of white marble, for self-knowledge and confession. The second is black, for contrition, mourning, and the reality of sin, and the third is blood-red for satisfaction — the Passion of Christ and our own penitence and acceptance of our share in satisfaction through suffering and good works. Having made his confession, Dante is admonished by Virgil to ask for absolution, entreating "most humbly of him to unlock the gate" (108). The angel draws out from under his ash-colored vestments the two keys, one of silver and one of gold. Keys of power and doom become humble instruments of everyday use, working together to open a door. It takes wit and skill to manipulate the keys. They stand for wisdom and patience, gentle virtues, not masterful ones. They symbolize the love and concern, learning and authority, that work together in the sacrament of reconciliation (or confession) to help the sinner recognize and name his or her true guilt, and be freed from false guilt. Deep down in each of us lies an accumulation of painful memories which can confuse and frighten us, and block us off from the forgiveness we long for. Sometimes it takes the fine-tuned ear of a good confessor to hear what we mean underneath the words we say in confession. Gentle skill in questioning is sometimes needed by the confessor (or the therapist) to bring the person to honest repentance. The silver key represents that skill, and the golden, more costly key (because bought with Christ's blood) stands for the priestly power of absolution. Together the keys unlock the gate and free the sinner.

In Canto 27 of *Paradiso*, Dante rages at Pope Boniface for using the symbol of the two keys on his war banners in the expedition against the Colonna family. Dante puts his rebuke in the mouth of St. Peter:

> Never by our intention was it willed
>
> ...that the keys bequeathed to me should stand
> As emblem on a banner waging war
> Against the baptized in a Christian land. (46-51)

As Dante moves through the gate of contrition and approaches the first ledge, the place where pride is cleansed, we have three pictures of the opposite virtue, humility, engraved upon the marble of the inner cliff. The first shows Mary, the mother of Jesus, at the Annunciation, while the second scene depicts David dancing before the Ark: "Before the sacred vessel, girded close,/His dancing feet the humble Psalmist plied,/And more than king in this and less he was" (10:64-6). The third scene shows the Emperor Trajan pausing in his cavalcade of mounted knights to listen to the grief of a poor woman. Daniel Berrigan comments, "A king, against all custom of great ones of this earth, turns aside from statecraft to hearken to 'the least of these.' For this he is remembered; for this, Dante honors him beyond measure."[29]

The images of humility and pardon come from Dante's own personal experience of daily life: the opening of a locked door when the bolt is rusty, the experience of rejection by his own city, and perhaps most painful of all, the experience of disappointment with the church as an institution symbolized by the papacy of Dante's day. These images spring also from the central illuminating image of his whole life: the image of Beatrice, her humility, her charity, and her power. In Beatrice a real, flesh and blood historical woman goes to him as a guide, accuser, provider, and rescuer. She is the inspiration for the whole of *The Divine Comedy*, which indeed embodies the central and final meaning of Dante's whole life.

Another passage about humility is from the third canto of *Paradiso*. His journey through the spheres takes Dante up, through those souls which are lowest even in heaven, to the highest souls. In the first ranges, "the slowest sphere," he meets Piccarda, a beautiful woman who had once been a nun but who had been forced by her brother to leave the convent and marry. She tells Dante that she is in the lowest place in heaven because she did "neglect and partly disavow her vow." Dante questions her: "But tell me, you whose happiness is here,/Have you no hankering to go up higher,/To win more insight or a love more dear?" (3:64-6). Piccarda explains her contentment with the well-known words, "His will is our peace."

> Brother, our love has laid our wills to rest,
> Making us long only for what is ours,
> And by no other thirst to be possessed....
>
> His will is our peace. (70-72, 85)

In this passage Piccarda finds peace through the submission of her will to the love of God. <u>Those who truly love God are entirely satisfied with God's will for them.</u> It is in accord with Paul's words in the Epistle to the Romans: "We know that in everything God works for good with those who love him" (8:28). Here, Christ "is our peace" because he shares with us the new creation, a new humanity, in which hostility and alienation have been overcome by his atoning death. In this passage from Dante the anagogical level is uppermost. The primary meaning of the passage has to do with our spiritual experience. An allegorical level of meaning, on the other hand, would relate it also to the historical and objective faith of the church. Perhaps, in fact, we need both if we are to understand "In his will is our peace" as it applies to us. Otherwise we can be left with an illusory ideal of peace as evasion of confrontation with our own inner strivings after autonomy and maturity. The passage from Ephesians leads us on to a corporate image of the church, its universal scope, and our call to stewardship within it.

In the course of the poem Virgil has accompanied Dante as his guide and mentor all the way down to the lowest pit of hell, and up and out again to the "sweet air." At the entrance of the earthly Paradise, Virgil announces the end of his mission as he says to Dante: "Await no further word or sign from me.../your will is free, erect and whole..../I crown and mitre you over yourself" (XXVII:139ff). Virgil has taken Dante as far as he can. Now Beatrice reappears and assumes the role of Dante's guide in the sphere of grace. He recognizes the love of his childhood, and "the strange outpouring power of hers/...the old, old love in all its mastering might" (XXX:37f). Dante turns to Virgil in this crisis of confrontation "as any little boy who ever came/running to mother with his fears and pains," but Virgil is not there: "O, he had left us, and we stood/orphaned of him...." And Dante weeps. We are not told whether Virgil returned to Limbo with the other "good pagans" or remained in the earthly Paradise in order to await the final resurrection.

It is Beatrice who meets Dante at the end of the *Purgatorio* and becomes his guide through the heavenly spheres. And yet she must first reproach and judge him.

> It would do violence to God's high doom
> If Lethe could be passed, and ill-doers
> To taste this blessed fare could straightway come
>
> Without some forfeit of repentant tears. (30:142-5)

"Repentant tears" are the sign of a changed heart. When we turn in sorrow from our false goals and acknowledge the truth of our sin and our need, we are open to God's cleansing grace. Turning and weeping, we meet the forgiveness of God.

In the *Paradiso* we see Beatrice's beauty and wisdom encourage Dante as he mounts toward the highest heavens. Her function is to lead him to the state whereby he can perceive beatitude and glory directly for himself. Before she leaves him, however, a remarkable thing happens. The steps and grades and spheres of heaven, distinctions of superior and inferior, cease to have any meaning. These symbols gradually fade and a new image appears, a river of light from which he must drink. Then Dante can behold the final vision. Beatrice explains to him that the blessed now move within that heaven which is pure light alone, where angels and the souls in bliss form God's court. There "near and far" have no meaning. As he looks, the river melts and changes into a snow-white rose. The heavenly court is surrounded by hosts of saints, and attended by angels who fly back and forth over the white petals of the rose like bees with golden wings.

But now he must part even from Beatrice. She has been the central illuminating image of his life. In this woman of flesh and blood, existing in time and space, he has found a guide, an accuser, a provider and a rescuer. She has not hesitated to judge him for his sins. She is his beatitude and his savior. From her he must part. Suddenly, like Virgil, she is no longer there, at his side, at his disposal. In this final deprivation when everything must have seemed lost, he is born anew and enters fully into his own autonomy.

A premature discarding of his guides, or a willful clinging to them after the time for parting had come, would have precipitated Dante back to the dreadful wood and the three beasts, and to the invitation to begin all over again at the beginning. Being "on our own" is supremely frightening,

and supremely cleansing and strengthening. It prepares us
for what we were created for: to behold God in the Holy
Trinity, and our own face there in the midst of it. Yet
Dante, after Beatrice leaves him, is given one more
intermediary in the figure of Bernard, the saint of
contemplation. St. Bernard calls upon the Virgin Mary: "O
Virgin Mother, Daughter of Thy Son...high noon of charity to
souls in bliss...Lady so great...." He asks her to pray that
Dante's sight may be so purified that he may attain the final
vision. Beatrice and all the saints join in her prayer, and
Bernard invites Dante to look upward toward the source of
all light, as Mary is looking: "Bernard conveyed to me what
I should do/By sign and smile: already on my own/I had
looked upwards, as he wished me to" (33:49-51). Even full
autonomy does not preclude courtesy, compliance, and
cooperation.

Dante's vision of the blessed in heaven brings him at last
to the heart of the Godhead. The ascent, when the highest
point is reached, becomes a circle, a community, and the
glory of one single light. Having passed through and beyond
Beatrice, Bernard, and the Virgin Mary, Dante comes at last
to that eternal light of the Trinity:

> That light supreme, within its fathomless
> Clear substance, showed to me three spheres, which
>   bare
> Three hues distinct, and occupied one space;
>
> The first mirrored the next, as though it were
> Rainbow from rainbow, and the third seemed
>   flame....
>
> The sphering thus begot, perceptible
> In Thee like mirrored light, now to my view —
> When I had looked on it a little while —
>
> Seemed in itself, and in its own self-hue,

Limned with our image.... (33:115-131)

Dante is puzzled. "The sphering thus begot" is the Son; the human features of Jesus are perceptible to Dante within the sphere. "So strove I with that wonder": he cannot grasp how to relate a human face, the face of Christ, to the face of the eternal Word and so reconcile the human and the divine.

St. Augustine's brief reference to the Trinity as the divine pattern which human beings, men and women, reflect was not developed in his writings. Dante picks up that theme here, but concludes his poem with the realisation that his own intellect was overwhelmed at the vision of love in the Holy Trinity. Words fail him. He can only say, in the concluding lines of the poem,

> My will and my desire were turned by love,
> The love that moves the sun and the other stars.

Throughout his life Dante's spirituality is faithful to the vision of love, and he comes at the end to see the oneness of his own human will and desire with the sovereign divine love of the triune God. It is through the image of a woman in her "holy and glorious flesh" that Dante comes to the vision of God, and finds there at its heart his own image. The poet offers us this same hope of finding, through one another, men and women, our own image at the heart of the Trinity. Humanity, concrete and particular in Beatrice, brings Dante to his own reality, to himself as reflecting God's image — made by God and for God. The image of God is revealed in *The Divine Comedy* through the experience of an earthly love. As we have seen, romantic love in the thirteenth century differs from what is commonly called "romance" today. It differs also from Augustine's love which longs to rise beyond earthly things and contemplate the eternal beauty of God, as well as from some of the ideas about love common in scholarly and courtly circles of Dante's world. Earthly love certainly did not exclude passion, but neither did it lead Dante to sexual union with his beloved. Dante never laments this fact. It was simply the case that a childhood encounter with the beauty and grace embodied in the child Beatrice became and remained for him supremely redemptive and transforming.

Dante's experience underlines for us the place of encounter as a meeting with the other, the opposite, as the place of rebirth. Through openness to risk, the risk of self-loss in our giving to and receiving from another, we find the image of our maker within our own hearts. It is our own face we see at the center of the Trinity, where the three persons of the Godhead live in the exchange of love.

Visions and Voices

Novices, in my first days in the convent, were not encouraged to dwell upon their inner experiences, and certainly not upon visions and voices. The first book I drew out of the convent library was the life of Teresa of Avila, but it was promptly removed from my hands and the *Life of Christ* by Jeremy Taylor was given me instead. Very prudent, too. First things do come first. Some obscure fascination with mysticism later drew me to sample the work of Julian of Norwich, her *Revelations of Divine Love*, as edited by Grace Warrack. It failed to hold my interest. I found the language too sweet, and the talk of love and suffering excessive. The idea of a woman being walled up alive in a small cell for the rest of her life repelled me. When I reread her many years later, however, I found her fresh and invigorating to a degree for which I was quite unprepared.

Visions and voices were generally accepted as emanating from God in the Hebrew and Christian scriptures as well as in much subsequent literature, both hagiography and spiritual theology. In Julian's time, while they were a commonplace of the tradition, they were viewed with some suspicion. False visions and false voices, not from God but from the devil, were as much feared and hated as true ones were valued and delighted in. A visionary could easily be suspected of being deluded by the devil and dragged into an ecclesiastical court on a charge of heresy.

Two centuries after Julian's time John of the Cross and Ignatius of Loyola gave some guidelines for distinguishing between authentic and inauthentic, and hence dangerous and deceptive, visions and voices. They still help us discern whether our own images and our "spiritual senses" come from God, or are merely echoes of our own will and desires or, worse yet, delusions and temptations from an evil spirit. The tests are twofold. Do these experiences speak to us of truths that conform to religion? Are they consistent with the teaching of Scripture and the church? What is their effect on our lives? Are we confused, excited, impressed with ourselves in consequence? Or are we conscious of a deeper peace, a greater love for others, and a more thorough-going humility?

"You will know them by their fruit," Jesus said. This is still the best test of authenticity.

In the nineteenth century, visionary experiences and biblical miracles were rejected as unscientific and hence impossible. In many Protestant countries and rationalist circles these experiences were regarded as signs of mental illness or superstition. Psychologists in more recent times have taken a fresh look at dreams and other psychological phenomena and seen them as messages from our own unconscious depths or from a collective unconscious — archetypes which symbolize universal human themes and drives. Some writers of spirituality regard "dream work" as an important way to recognize spiritual realities, and others urge caution because of the dangers of self-preoccupation and grandiosity which can invest the products of our own imagination with universal meaning and divine significance. The ancient rules of discernment still apply. Moreover, visions and voices are not the substance of the experience of God, but rather accidental features which may or may not accompany divine revelations.

Julian's visions are a mixed lot. Some of them, such as the parable of the Lord and the servant, are beautiful and profoundly moving, yielding rich illuminations when they are explored. Others are ugly and convey only disgust, such as her description of the devil with a brick-red face and black freckles. Some are homely, derived from everyday

experiences, like the scales of a herring or water dripping
from eaves; still others are highly symbolic, like her vision of
a hazelnut in the palm of her hand. Nearly all of these
visions, for me and for many people today, seem to
demonstrate how the psychological experiences of a woman
can give us new ways of thinking about God. It is not the
visions themselves that interest Julian, but what they teach
her about God's love. In the solitary instance of which we
have a record, she does not refer to her visionary experience
when counseling another woman, but to its content, its
meaning. In what follows we shall be looking at her struggle
to interpret her "showings" and the problem they pose in
seeming to contradict church doctrine. We will be looking
for the substance of her visions and voices, for their
consonance with the truth of the gospel and their relevance to
our own experience.

Julian was a fourteenth-century English anchoress, a
professed religious who was not necessarily the member of a
religious order. She lived alone with one or two attendants in
a small dwelling attached to a parish church in Norwich, a
provincial center which London alone surpassed in population
and wealth. She would have had a little garden and a few
rooms for living purposes, but she would not have had free
access to the world outside nor the world to her. Her
enclosure prevented that. Julian's house would have had two
windows, one looking into the church, through which she
could join in parish worship; the other closed with a curtain
when not in use, and facing out upon the world. Through
this window she would have been able to talk to those who
came to her for counsel. It must have been something like
being locked into a few Sunday school rooms and a vestry,
with a back door opening onto an acre or so of land where a
few onions and cabbages, peas and beans and turnips, could
grow.

Julian's time would have been spent in solitary prayer, in assisting at the parish mass, and in household and garden tasks: weeding, gardening, feeding the cat, shelling peas, with an attendant to do the outside errands and give a hand with the work. Such visitors as came for spiritual counsel were received, as the Benedictine rule directed, as Christ himself. Gossip and trivialities were not encouraged. Julian would have had some kind of rule of life, perhaps one of the current rules for anchoresses. There were Augustinian friars in Norwich in her day, not far from the anchorhold, and the rule of Augustine might have had some influence in her life, but we know nothing for certain about her spiritual and intellectual formation beyond what can be inferred from her book, *The Revelations of Divine Love.*

There were many recluses, both men and women, in medieval England. They seem indeed to have been almost the only source of spiritual direction for lay people, beyond the limitations of the parish clergy. Julian is remembered because of her book, which she wrote to describe the series of visions given to her during one day, Sunday, May 13, 1373, and the following night, and her reflection upon them during the next twenty years. She understood her vocation to prayer to include and even to center upon the "comfort and help of my even-Christians." She gives us a generalized account of her visions and draws out the meaning, not for her own edification or to claim a place in history, but for its usefulness to others. The imagery of these visions was deeply rooted in the traditional piety of the parish and the monastery which was her heritage. But, most importantly, they arise naturally from her own personal depths.

Her spirituality and her theology are based upon her experience and her reflections upon it, no doubt in dialogue with her confessor, rather than upon systematic teaching such as she might have received in a monastic house of her time. The visions were given, she tells us, in response to a certain prayer, a prayer that she came later to regret a little and, in the end, to reinterpret. Here is the prayer: "...I desired three graces by the gift of God. The first was to have recollection of Christ's Passion. The second was a bodily sickness, and the third was to have, of God's gift, three wounds....the wound of contrition, the wound of compassion, and the wound of longing with my will for God."[30]

All three graces are described in terms of poverty and humility. They do not reflect the normal content of human wishes for health and comfort, riches and success. The first grace, seeing Christ's passion, was an experience so costly that it nearly brought her death in the bodily sickness which accompanied the showings, and which she asked for. She came to doubt the prudence of having asked for such graces: "Thinking that if I had known what it had been, I should have been reluctant to ask for it." She never regretted the third request, which was for a triple poverty: the spiritual poverty of self-knowledge and contrition, the poverty of ego-loss in the going out of herself in compassion, identifying herself with the neediness and insufficiency of others, and the deeper poverty of spiritual thirst — longing for God who is absent.

Julian understood her visions as being given (as all charisms are, ordination, prophesy, tongues, as well as visions) *for others*, and not for herself. She learned from her visions how to look upon the sins of others, and, of course, in particular, how to regard the sins and weaknesses and failings, the neediness and the vulnerability, of those who came to her for counsel. We are to contemplate another's sin, she says, "with contrition with him, with compassion on him, and with holy desires to God for him" (p. 328). This is the working out, in pastoral terms, of the three wounds. It is a wholesome pattern still, for loving our enemies, for hearing confessions or apologies, for praying for others, and for the giving of spiritual counsel.

Many of Julian's sayings and images are arresting. They stick in the mind. They have also outraged some of her readers. Julian has never been canonized, and some say it is because her teaching about sin is not orthodox, such as when

she writes, "I saw no kind of wrath in God," or "I did not
see sin, for I believe that it has no kind of substance, no
share in being, nor can it be recognized except by the pain
caused by it" (pp. 264, 225). Let us listen to this woman,
perhaps the greatest theologian of the fourteenth century, and
to her message for our own time. Everything she said is
within the context of her twenty years of meditation upon
those visions of the passion of Jesus, which were given once
and for all in May, 1373. From this single experience, a
succession of sixteen "showings" and her long reflection upon
them, all her teaching springs.

From Julian's ponderings on her visions of Christ's
passion, then, there emerges a rich and complex spirituality
which combines in a remarkable way orthodoxy and
optimism. The mystics are often accused of not taking sin
and evil seriously enough, and indeed Julian was suspected of
heresy in having too high a view of the human soul, and too
cheerful an assurance that "all shall be well" for every soul
God has made. We should take Julian's teaching as a whole,
however, set as it is in the single perspective of her vision of
the Passion and its cause in human sin.

Julian's themes, her theological reflections upon her
visions, are interwoven rather than consecutive. The central
theme is love — God's unconditional love for his creatures.
Linked with this in an organic way are other themes: the
mystery of sin, the Holy Trinity, the motherhood of God,
Mary the mother of Jesus, prayer. Each of her themes
springs from her visions and her meditations upon the
visions. They unfold, open out, from the central vision of
the Passion of Jesus to the vision of God as Holy Trinity.
Her account is straightforward but not simplistic — it is in
fact highly compact and complex — as she tries to share her
gifts, insights and inspirations with her fellow Christians.
Love is the dominating theme, and her images are in its
service. Creation, sin, the Trinity, the Mother of God,
ourselves, all appear in relation to love. The organization is
based not upon objective analysis, but first of all upon the

visions themselves and then upon the natural flow of her imagination as she employed it to record and interpret those visions.

I would like to look at each of these themes, beginning with God's love for all creatures. The well-known vision of the hazelnut in the fifth chapter of her *Revelations* leads us to the heart of her teaching about God's love for all that has been created:

> At the same time as I saw this sight of the head
> bleeding, our good Lord showed a spiritual sight
> of his familiar love....And in this he showed me
> something small, no bigger than a hazelnut, lying
> in the palm of my hand, as it seemed to me, and it
> was as round as a ball. I looked at it with the eye
> of my understanding and thought: What can this
> be? I was amazed that it could last, for I thought
> that because of its littleness it would suddenly
> have fallen into nothing. And I was answered in my
> understanding; It lasts and always will, because
> God loves it; and thus everything has being through
> the love of God. (p. 183)

Here Julian gives us a fresh view of creation coming forth from God, held in being by love — a concept which puts me in mind of the lovely statue of God creating Adam, from the north porch of Chartres Cathedral. It is very different from Michelangelo's powerful fresco at the Vatican, all maleness and muscle. The Chartres creator cradles Adam's head with his hand and looks down at his earth-creature with such love and joy!

The mystery of sin is never far from the mystery of love in Julian. She says some astonishing things about this, some of which we have already noticed, such as, "I saw no kind of wrath in God," and more surprising still, "Between God and our soul there is neither wrath nor forgiveness in his sight" (p. 259). Julian's difficulty is evident. Her visions spoke to her of divine love and spoke so clearly that she could never in any way deny them. In this she resembles the young Joan of Arc, almost her contemporary, who never, even to the point of death by fire, denied or gave up her "voices." Julian's fire was not an English pyre, but rather the pyres of an English hell. She was caught between the revelations which showed her the love and mercy in the everlastingness of God, and the teaching of the church of her day, where the possibility for sinners of everlasting torment in hell and the wrath of God against sinners was conveyed in sermons, and also visually in many forms. The "Mouth of Hell" was often part of the stage setting of morality plays, for instance. Medieval cathedrals often used the theme of the last judgment in the sculptures of their western portals to bring this teaching, in its concrete horror, home to all who entered. We have already seen how concretely Dante understood and accepted the punishment of sinners in hell. Over and over again Julian tells us how she is torn apart by opposites: the love and mercy of a God who does not blame and is not angry, and the traditional belief in judgment and eternal punishment.

She could not be fully comforted, she says, as she reflects on her showings. Her solution, which is really no more a solution than was Job's, is found in the long parable of the Lord and the servant, in chapter fifty-one of the long text (pp. 267ff). She describes the Lord as sitting on the earth in a desert place, clothed in a flowing blue garment, "fair but not gaudy." He had dark eyes, beautiful and filled with pity and "within him a high world, long and broad, all full of endless heavenliness." The servant who stood before him wore only a workman's tunic, short and stained, dirtied from a fall into a deep ravine. The Lord looked upon the servant, Julian says, with a constant merciful love, especially in his falling. This pity which the Father shows for his son is both the pity of the eternal God for Adam his fallen creature, and the joy and bliss for the falling of his most dear Son into the womb of the Virgin — the Son who is equal with himself. The anchoress explains that we must not conclude from this that God is a man, or that he sits literally in a barren place of the earth. His sitting means that God has taken our soul for his constant dwelling place. The endless merciful love with which he beholds his servant shows how God looks upon sinful men and women. He is never discouraged or turned aside from this love and this purpose to dwell intimately with his creatures. He has "more joy in his all-love and sorrow in our frequent fallings."

Much of medieval piety reflects a spirit of despair and shame over the sinfulness of our fleshly life. In Julian's vision we are one with the lowly servant, who is both Son and Adam, that is, all of us, and in him we are dearly loved just as we are, in our woeful state, and never blamed by the dear Lord who sits so meekly on the earth in a barren place, and is our God.

In the end, Julian lives with the tension between what her showings reveal and the teachings of the church. Thomas Merton comments on this: "She must indeed believe and accept the fact that there is a hell, yet also at the same time, impossibly, one would think, she believes even more firmly that 'the word of Christ shall be saved in all things,' and 'all manner of thing shall be well.' This is, for her, the heart of theology: not solving the contradiction, but remaining in the midst of it, in peace, knowing that it is fully solved, but that the solution is secret and will never be guessed at until it is revealed."[31]

The problem of mercy and judgment also led Julian into her doctrine of the Holy Trinity and of our creation in its image; "We were made like the Trinity in our first making." In this she echoes Augustine, Bernard and Dante, although she had little chance of access to the first two and none at all to the last. Julian expands this idea more concretely than any of her predecessors. As she prayed over and pondered on the parable of the Lord and the servant, she saw that our relationship to God was trinitarian: "I saw and understood that the high might of the Trinity is our Father, and the deep

wisdom of the Trinity is our Mother, and the great love of
the Trinity is our Lord; and all these we have in nature" (p.
294). Julian saw that motherhood as well as fatherhood is
predicated of God, for "the second person of the Trinity is
our Mother in nature in our substantial creation, in whom we
are founded and rooted, and he is our Mother of mercy in
taking our sensuality."

Julian describes the relationship between the Holy
Trinity and the soul in bridal imagery: "And so I saw that
God rejoices that he is our Father and God rejoices that he is
our Mother, and God rejoices that he is our true spouse, and
that our soul is his beloved wife" (p. 279). She also sees that
in our sensuality as well as our spirituality we are capable of
union with God and reflect God. Her insight here is close to
Dante's, when he sees in the goodness, wisdom and beauty of
a concrete, fleshly girl, Beatrice Portinari, the fundamental
inspiration of his life. Her further understanding of the
motherhood of God makes possible a needed corrective to the
anthropology of Augustine and Aquinas, neither of whom
granted that women, autonomously and equally with men, are
created in the image of God.

Julian brought the theme of motherhood also to her
understanding of the passion of Jesus. While the Gospel of
John finds in the brazen serpent that Moses made and set
upon a pole a type of Jesus on the cross, for Julian it is the
most feminine of all symbols, the womb, which is a metaphor
of the cross. Julian says, "In his blessed dying on the Cross
he bore us to endless life." Through the identification of
Jesus our Mother with our bodily life as well as our spiritual
life, the whole of our experience, including the aspects
usually reserved for women, can express the divine life. Our
feelings and relationships, female or male, masculine or
feminine, can become signs and channels for the love of God.
Julian looks also at God as mother, and describes this womb
love for us: "And since that time, now and even until the
day of judgment, he feeds us and fosters us, just as the
supreme lovingness of motherhood wishes, and as the natural

need of childhood asks" (p. 304). She may be echoing here the words that Paul uses in I Corinthians, "I fed you with milk, not solid food, for you were not ready for it" (3:2,3), or the text of I Peter, "Like newborn babes, long for the pure spiritual milk that you may grow up to salvation; for you have tasted the kindness of the Lord" (2:2).

Julian is best known, perhaps, for her theological optimism. Her famous saying, "All shall be well, and all shall be well, and all manner of things shall be well," is often quoted, but perhaps with little understanding of what soul-searching anguish it cost her to maintain it. She is known also, in a vague way, for having given a special place to the feminine aspect of God: "So Jesus Christ, who opposes good to evil, is our true Mother. We have our being from him, where the foundation of motherhood begins" (p. 295). This expresses perhaps the essence of Julian's teaching about who we are, creatures made in the divine image. We are all, female and male alike, borne from the womb of love, of God. Julian was not a "feminist," of course, in the modern sense. When she speaks of Jesus as our mother, she does not shudder at also calling Jesus "he" in the same sentence. She is not concerned with the feminine as such, but simply with fidelity to her visions.

All the more telling, therefore, is her teaching about those qualities which, although they are regarded as feminine and inferior and not highly valued or rewarded in society to this day, are nevertheless especially needed if we are to preserve life on this planet and find ways of living creatively with those who are different. We need the recognition and acceptance of our vulnerability and dependence, frankness about the body, concern for human development, empathy and a nurturing patience with others. Her visions of the Passion and the parable of the Lord and the servant describe the weakness and woundedness of the Son (who is also Adam, the earth creature) as drawing out the deepest love and respect and joy of the Father. Her frankness about the body is shown in a curious passage about our basic biological function of elimination as God's way of serving us "in the simplest natural functions of our body." This is very different from much of the tradition that denigrates the body and sees it as a sack of filth.

Though she seldom uses bridal imagery, which so many of the mystics do in speaking of the relationship of the soul with God, she does not hesitate to use sexual imagery to describe God's love for us. In the images of both loves, married love and the love of friendship, she is not far from such earlier writers as Aelred of Rievaulx in his treatise *On Spiritual Friendship*, and from Dante.

Julian approaches the subject of prayer through her own experience of dryness and barrenness, an experience she shares with all who feel that after prayer they are the same sorry selves they were before — that nothing has happened. She writes, "And Our Lord brought all this suddenly to my mind, and revealed these words and said: I am the ground of your beseeching" (p. 248). Beseeching, she tells us, is itself the union of our will with the will of our Lord by the will of our Lord by the operation of the Holy Spirit, and our Lord accepts it thankfully. These are two comforting and invigorating propositions: the work of prayer is the work of God in us; and God is glad when we pray, however dry and barren we may feel. Prayer itself is an image of the life of God in us.

Julian goes on to say that thanksgiving is a part of prayer, as it is of any human relationship, and she sums up her teaching in three points: our prayer originates in the love and will and specific intention of God; our prayer is united to and sustained by the divine energy of our Lord's own prayer; through our prayer we are made like our Lord in all things. She cautions us not to try to make God "supple and obedient to us," but to make ourselves supple and obedient to God. Finally, she speaks again of the activity of prayer as reflecting God: "The endless supreme truth, endless supreme wisdom, endless supreme love" of our creator. "And always it does what it was created for; it sees God, and it contemplates God, and it loves God" (p. 256).

    Julian's discernment and pastoral concern for others is demonstrated by her dealings with Margery Kempe, whom del Mastro describes as a "vivid, unusual, and according to most of her contemporaries, peculiar woman." Margery gives her own account of her visit to Julian, and here is some of Margery's story:

> Then she was bidden by our Lord to go to an
> anchoress in the same city [Norwich], named
> Dame Jelyen....The anchoress, hearing the
> marvelous goodness of our Lord, highly thanked
> God with all her heart for His visitation,
> counselling this creature to be obedient to
> the will of our Lord and to fulfill with all
> her might whatever he put into her soul, if
> it were not against the worship of God, and
> profit of her fellow Christians, for if it
> were, then it were not the moving of a good
> spirit, but rather of an evil spirit....[32]

Here we see that Julian has her own test for the discernment of spirits. Then Margery quotes Julian directly: "Holy Writ saith that the soul of a rightful man is the seat of God, and so I trust, sister, that ye be. Set all your trust in God and fear not the language of the world...patience is necessary for you, for in that shall ye keep your soul." Julian's words to this troubled, illiterate, and perhaps hysterical woman had to do only with Margery and her experience, her fears and her questions. There is no sign that in her converse with Margery Julian ever referred to her own experiences or writings.

    What was Julian's reaction to the attitude to women in the culture and the church of her day? As far as the church in England during the fourteenth century was concerned, bias against women was enshrined in its canon law, its liturgy and rubrics, its theology, and its folklore.

In the writings of Julian, as in *The Ancrene Riwle*, there is evident an awareness of the text of I Corinthians 14, which bade women be silent in church and ask their husbands at home if they wanted to know something (14:35-6). *The Ancrene Riwle* bids the anchoress "imitate our Lady and not cackling Eve." It forbids her "to preach to any man; nor must any man ask of you or give you advice or counsel; consult with women only."[33] "*Mulieres non permitto docere*," "I do not allow women to teach," was believed to have been written by St. Paul. So Julian excuses herself from appearing to preach: "Because I am a woman, ought I therefore to believe that I should not tell you of the goodness of God, when I saw at that same time that is his will that it be known? Then will you soon forget me who am a wretch, and do this, so that I am no hindrance to you, and you will contemplate Jesus, who is every man's teacher" (p. 135). So she writes in the Short Text. In the longer text, written years later, she does not repeat this defensive justification. Perhaps in the interval Julian grew more serene and sure of her calling to share her revelations with her "even-Christians" of both sexes, for she makes no distinction between men and women.

Throughout Christian history women actually have had a recognized teaching role in the church as deaconesses, as women who converted their husbands to Christianity, as prophets, mystics, writers of letters and learned treatises of many subjects. We have seen that Gregory of Nyssa called his sister Macrina, "Teacher." So it seems that women studied, learned and taught, on the one hand, and the medieval church officially denied them the right to the title "Teacher," on the other hand. Only in our century were Catherine of Siena and Teresa of Avila accorded the title "Doctor of the Church." Jean LeClerq comments, "Each society needs models...our times require feminine models." If the church had remained "a masculine stronghold it would have been limited and partial. It would have missed the characteristic genius of the feminine with its intuitive approach to reality. In relation to God this is the only effective approach."[34]

Just as Julian was able to hold on to two incompatible truths as she saw them, that God punished sinners in hell and that there was no wrath or punishment in God, so she was able, as many other women were, to remain a loyal, obedient, humble daughter of the church as she understood it and at the same time to speak with autonomy, clearly and bravely, about the things she believed God had revealed to her in visions and prayer. Thomas Merton says of her: "I pray much to have a wise heart, and perhaps the discovery of Lady Julian of Norwich will help me. I took her book with me on a quiet walk among the cedars. She is a true theologian with greater clarity, depth, and order than St. Teresa: she really elaborates, theologically, the content of her revelations. She first experienced, then thought, and the thoughtful deepening of her experience worked it back into her life, deeper and deeper, until her whole life as a recluse at Norwich was simply a matter of getting completely saturated in the light she had received all at once, in the 'shewings,' when she thought she was about to die."[35]

It takes courage to say "all will be well, all manner of thing shall be well." And she who said it first learned it by contemplating suffering, not by hiding from it — the suffering of the Son of God, who is also our mother.

We have seen that Julian's whole work proceeded from the series of visions she received on a day in May. These visions or "showings" impressed her with their givenness, although the words she heard were in the English of her day, and the images she saw were derived from her ordinary experience. She had certainly seen the scales of herring, rain dripping from eaves, hazelnuts in their shells, and recognized lords and servants from their dress. The givenness had to do with their meaning, and that meaning she drew from the visions by long years of reflection and prayer, questioning

and reasoning about them. The longer text of her
Revelations, an expanded version of the short text, in-
corporates her more mature and seasoned understanding of
the messages God had given her.

This very process is a meeting. We think today that the
activity of creative imagination proceeds from the right side
of the brain, and that its fluid images are rationalized,
ordered and interpreted by the left side of the brain. Julian
was faithful to this double process, and to her intellectual as
well as her intuitive gifts. Together they produced her
Revelations of Divine Love.

The images of God which she gives us often come
specifically from her own experience as a woman. They give
us new metaphors which balance and enlarge the masculine
metaphors which abound in the Christian tradition. Julian
does not force these feminine images on us, nor does she use
them for apology or polemics. Some of her images are
masculine: God is a lord and a king, as well as a city and a
mother. Just as she is willing to live with the apparent
contradiction between the church's teaching about the wrath
of God and God's own words to her about mercy, she is able
to keep together masculine and feminine images and see them
as pointing toward one reality.

Even in the most perfect of human meetings, there seems
to be an element which is not susceptible to assimilation on
either side. This element may seem like an obscurity or a
shadow or a seed of dissolution. It keeps us open to the truth
of our incompletion, and to the possibility of more light and
further development in our living and our dying.

The basic image of meeting is the Holy Trinity itself, a
meeting of one another in a mutuality and exchange of self-
giving love. As Augustine suggests and Dante illustrates with
his three circles, Julian also sees and asserts: "The blessed
Trinity made mankind in their image" (p. 194). It is a
dynamic pattern, pointing to our human experience of
community, our acceptance of one another as different yet all
alike, equally worthy of love.

Contemporary Metaphors

In the chapter that follows we shall be looking at the themes my introduction promised to deal with, themes related to our experience of and our search for clues to the divine image in human beings. These themes concern the Holy Trinity as the basic pattern of human experience and the place of feeling, instinct, passion, and sexuality — no less than intellect and will — in reflecting the energy of God as Holy Trinity. We begin to see the emergence of a perceptible movement away from patriarchal values and presuppositions toward something new. That "something" has not yet entirely emerged and we can only guess at what it will be and do. Changes in technology and communications, new discoveries in the fields of science and psychology, have opened vast new possibilities for human life, not all of them beneficent. Perhaps Christians today are called to explore and to discriminate more than to evangelize, or else to find new ways to evangelize.

Each of us, in our measure, makes what casts we can into the unknown, the future opening before us, and brings back tokens from our encounters there: a bunch of grapes, so large it must be carried by two people; a stone with a strange shape; a mysterious herb; a golden bough or a jewelled bird; an incantation in a lost tongue; a diagram or a map, marked with an X.

It is a large order, and one I can address myself to only in fear and trembling. A few mornings ago I awoke with a line of my own creating, running in my head: "I am a very small potato in a various stew."

When I was still a junior professed sister, much troubled by doubts and questions, the key which was to unlock so many rusty doors and open for me a way into a new understanding of Scripture, of theology, and of myself, was given to me by Frank Gavin. He was a priest and doctor of the church, and a friend of the sisters of the order I had joined. I was a fervent sponge in those days, soaking up doctrine and liturgy, and trying to learn to pray according to some highly recommended "methods." After a year and a half in the novitiate, with six months to go before first annual vows, I was sent back to school by my community to Boston University to complete my undergraduate work in the classics. It was during the years of the Great Depression. On my way to classes, walking through Boston Common, I was confronted morning after morning with the sight of men wrapped in newspapers and sleeping on park benches, or huddled at the subway entrance for warmth. The sight struck home to me, to my heart. Each morning I arose earlier than I liked, from a bed that was narrow but warm and clean, and before I set out for school I ate an adequate breakfast. What on earth did I mean by a vow of poverty? I was not poor as these men, and a few women, were. Was poverty a *good*, that I should vow it? Or an evil, that I should do something about?

Reflections like these, together with courses in anthropology, history, philosophy and economics, all part of the required program for a degree in the College of Liberal Arts, challenged my faith and brought me to a vocational crisis.

I was still unsettled when I was sent to Kentucky to be part of a new foundation there and to help reopen Margaret Hall School in Versailles. In the summer of 1933 Father Frank Gavin came to us to give us our long retreat, and to be the "headliner" for the diocesan summer conference which was held at the school. He was a professor of Church History at the General Theological Seminary in New York, and in 1937, the year before his death, he became Warden of the Kentucky convent. It was that retreat and those lectures, together with some personal interviews with him, that began to open doors and set me on a new course as a Christian believer and as a religious. They also formed the basis for my subsequent work of teaching Christian Doctrine at Margaret Hall School.

The retreat was formative for my understanding of the relationship between doctrine and social action. His topic was the Holy Trinity as a pattern of the divine life and for every form of human community. My problem about the meaning of poverty was not resolved, but at least I had found a context for thinking about it. He gave two series of lectures at the conference, one in the evenings, on the Hebrew prophets, and one in the mornings, on the Apostles' Creed. The evening lectures introduced me to the critical study of Scripture. It was an intensely exhilarating and liberating experience. No longer must I try to stifle or argue away my doubts and difficulties. Instead I began to respect my questions, and work through them if I could, with the help of whatever contemporary scholarship I had access to. The morning series freed me likewise from a cut-and-dried approach to theology. We began to study the creed from the end, with "Amen," and worked backwards, finally arriving at the most difficult and demanding article: "I believe in God." "Amen," Fr. Gavin said, meant in Hebrew, "so be it," and stood for the "acceptive attitude," a temper of mind which is open to new challenges and new ideas, willing to listen, to test, hospitable but also discriminating. It was a liberating approach to theology.

In his personal counsel to me, also, Fr. Gavin was equally stimulating and liberating. He did not hesitate to be tough. He encouraged me never to be afraid of the truth, but to follow it wherever it might lead, even if it led me out of the church. God is the author of truth, and if I followed the truth as I honestly saw it, the spirit would lead me in the end to God. Then he delivered his final thrust: "It will be worse

before it is better. I don't know whether you have the guts
to go through with it or not."

Whether he knew it or not, this was the kind of dare an
adolescent young nun like me in those days could not resist.
He followed up his counsel with recommendations on what to
read, beginning with *Lux Mundi* (which became bread and
meat to me in those days), and the promise to continue
listening and helping me in the days ahead. So he became
for me a key to open new perspectives and a pivot to help
me turn in a new direction without breaking my contact with
the past.

These convictions of mine that underlie my interpretation
of Scripture and theology stem from that summer's
experience. The first is the insight and conviction that the
holiness to which we are called is corporate, and the Holy
Trinity is the pattern of human relationships. That is to say,
mutual self-giving life is the pattern of the inner life of God,
and is reflected in us, in all our relationships, when we open
ourselves to it as gift and grace.

The second is the conviction that the flesh with its
desires and drives, is holy. Sexuality is a reflection of the
love of God in the Trinity, and it reflects that life in us.

Finally, our minds are good, made by God for truth.
Faith is not opposed to truth. We must never be afraid of
new expressions of truth. Trusting in God makes sense, more
sense than not trusting in God. Difficulties serve to test and
refine our fidelity to our Christian vocation.

In light of these convictions about God and ourselves, I
look briefly in the closing chapter at the present scene for
signs of a spirituality for a human future.

A great cultural gap separates us not only from Gregory,
Augustine, Dante and Julian, but also from the spiritual
guides of the early part of our own century. Discoveries in
depth psychology and the behavioral sciences, such as the
importance of unconscious motivation and the need to take

seriously our own feelings, have affected our understanding
of the spiritual life. Theology also has moved away from
dependence on authoritative propositions toward a larger
measure of acceptance for new ways of expressing traditional
doctrines.

I shall look at some examples from current fiction,
spirituality, and theology for some fresh metaphors for the
themes this book has addressed. Human beings were created
to reflect the mutuality of love and respect which exists
between the persons of the Trinity. Our relationships with
the other, women with men, friend with friend, the human
being with the rest of creation, should point toward our
divine origin. We shall take another look at qualities once
considered to be stronger by nature in women than in men,
but which are capable of equally creative development in
persons of either gender. As we have seen, such qualities
have often been suppressed or devalued in the tradition of
Christian spirituality and in our culture generally, but they
are especially needed in the world we live in today. They
include vulnerability, the patience and love required for long-
term nurturing and healing, the capacity for making
connections between persons and creating new forms of
community, and a positive attitude toward the body and
toward sexuality. Finally, I shall point to some fresh images
of encounter, of meeting, of the bringing together of
opposites in fruitful ways.

We shall look first at some current fiction. Descriptions
and instances of the human capacity for vulnerability and
woundedness abound and sometimes seem to dominate the
literary scene. And T. S. Eliot, of course, was right — we
cannot bear very much reality so we take refuge in distortion
and exaggeration as in horror stories, and in illusion as in
advertising and pornography.

Vulnerability is described by Alice Walker in her novel,
The Color Purple in such graphic detail, with such a wealth
and weight of concrete instance and inexorability, that one
can hardly bear to read the book through. The story is

written in the form of letters that the protagonist, Celie, writes to God and to her sister. Celie is a 14 year-old black girl living in the deep South. She has been raped continuously by her stepfather, himself a victim of racial prejudice and economic exploitation. The resulting babies are murdered by their father, and Celie is effectively locked into her situation by his warning: "You better not tell nobody but God. It'd kill your mommy."[36] She accepts his suggestion and addresses herself to God in letters.

The woman who eventually becomes a deliverer for Celie, Shug Avery, is the lover of the man Celie is forced to marry. The women become friends and confidants rather than rivals, and Celie confides to Shug her doubts about the God to whom she has been telling her story:

"Ain't no way to read the Bible," she explains, "and not think God white. When I found out I thought God was white, I lost interest." She no longer writes letters to God, but to her lost sister, Nettie.

Shug responds by describing her own alienation from this white God, and her breakthrough to a new understanding of God, a new acceptance of herself and her experience.

"My first step from the old white man was trees. Then air. Then birds. Then other people. But one day when I was sitting quiet and feeling like a motherless child, which I was, it come to me: that feeling of being part of everything, not separate at all."

Shug teaches Celie that God loves feeling, including sexual feelings.

"God love all them feelings. That's some of the best stuff God ever did...God love everything you love....I think it pisses God off if you walk by the color purple in a field somewhere and don't notice it."

Celie's deliverance from self-hatred comes first, and then her deliverance from fear and hatred for her former tormentor and victimizer, whom she calls "Mr. _____."

"My skin dark. My nose just a nose. My lips just lips. My body just any woman's body going through the changes of age. Nothing special here for nobody to love. No honey colored curly hair, no cuteness. Nothing young and fresh. My heart must be young and fresh, though, it feels like it blooming blood." When she meets Mr. _____, now old and alone, they talk a little about the past. Celie writes about him in a letter to her sister, Nettie:

"After all the evil he done I know you wonder why I don't hate him. I don't hate him for two reasons. One, he loves Shug. Two, Shug used to love him. Plus he look like he trying to make something out of himself. I don't mean just that he work and he clean up after himself and he appreciates some of the things God was playful enough to make. I mean when you talk to him now he really listen, and one time, out of nowhere, in the conversation us was having, he said Celie, I'm satisfied. This is the first time I ever lived in Earth as a natural man. It feel like a new experience."

The story ends with Celie and old Mr. _____ at peace with one another. Mr. _____ speaks of himself as "the fool I used to be." Celie replies:

"Well, I say, we all have to start somewhere if us want to do better, and our own self is what we have to hand."

...

"Then the old devil put his arms around me and just stood there on the porch with me real quiet. Way after while I bent my stiff neck onto his shoulder. Here us is, I thought, two old fools left over from love, keeping each other company under the stars."

What does Alive Walker's story have to tell us about vulnerability? First, it does not say that vulnerability is good, or healing, by itself. The capacity for suffering, for woundedness is characteristic of sentient beings as such. It is necessary for our survival and for our development as persons, able to feel and love and give of ourselves to others. If the burnt child dreads the fire, the child who has not been burned does not know what fire is, and can neither guard against its destructive power nor help others in danger from it.

Vulnerability is not healing in itself. If there is a "wounded healer," to use Henri Nouwen's image, there is also Typhoid Mary. Nouwen makes the wounded healer the focus of his reflections on ministry in the book by that name, and says, "The minister is called to recognize the sufferings of his time in his own heart and make that recognition the starting point of his service."[37] Typhoid Mary was a woman who carried the deadly germs of typhoid fever in her body without suffering the disease herself. She was a "carrier," dangerous and infectious to others, without awareness of her own state. She is the dark side, the shadow, of the wounded healer.

How do we keep our own wounds from being infectious rather than healing? Julian of Norwich gave us counsel about this when she said we are to pray for a sinner in three stages —"with contrition with him, with compassion on him, and with holy desires to God for him" (p. 328). Typhoid Mary cannot have "contrition with" anyone, for she has no awareness of her own need for healing. Celie, in Walker's story, must begin with her own heart and must recognize and accept its woundedness. As long as the God she prays to is himself an oppressor, the "white man God," who like the town mayor, "never listen to what the colored said," her self-acceptance is false. She accepts hopelessness, inferiority, blame. When her friend Shug is able to convince her to give up this white man God, and accept her own being as good, she begins to move out of her imprisonment. She is conscious of her vulnerability, but she is also conscious of her own reality; her own heart, as part of all reality, and she accepts her "own self as what we have to hand." She takes Julian's second step, compassion, when she moves out toward Mr. _____ in kindness. She turns the painful point of his self-inflicted judgment, "The fool I used to be," with the reply, "We all have to start somewhere if us want to do better."

Celie's third step is not expressed as a "holy desire to

God for him," but in her recognition and acceptance of a
new relationship: "Two old fools left over from love,
keeping each other company under the stars." Like
Nouwen's wounded healer, she has recognized the sufferings
of her time in her own heart, and used the recognition in
service to another person, to reestablish relationship and to
make peace.

Celie's last letter is addressed to God:
"Dear God. Dear stars, dear trees, dear sky, dear
peoples. Dear Everything. Dear God."

Another contemporary writer who speaks about
vulnerability is Annie Dillard. Her brief story, *Holy the
Firm*, deals with the affront and the mystery of innocent
suffering — the suffering of a child.[38] She places us at once
in her own house on northern Puget Sound, with its views of
mountains and sea, and says:

"I came here to study hard things, rock, mountain and
salt sea — and to temper my spirit on their hard edges.
'Teach me Thy ways, O Lord' is, like all prayers, a rash one,
and one I cannot but recommend." She does not spare
herself or us when she describes a terrible accident to a small
child. Is there an echo there of Julian of Norwich and her
prayer for the experience of suffering?

"Into this world falls a plane...I heard it go...and Julie
Norwich seven years old burnt off her face." Not for nothing
is the child named Julie Norwich. Just as Julian faces into
the immediate horror of physical pain and disfigurement
shown her in the visions of Christ's passion, so in *Holy the
Firm* Dillard faces into the terrible mystery of the suffering
of children. She shows us first that it must be confronted.

"Little Julie mute in some room at St. Joe's now, drugs
dissolving into the sheets. Little Julie with her eyes naked,
and spherical, baffled. Can you scream without lips? Yes.
But do children in long pain scream?"

Dillard gives tongue to her own rage.

"Of faith I have nothing, only of truth: that this one
God is a brute and a traitor, abandoning us to time, to

necessity, and the engines of matter unhinged...one Julie, one
sorrow, one sensation bewildering the heart and enraging the
mind, and causing me to look at the world stuff appalled...."
She discards faith in a God who created all things and then
withdrew, yet she also suggests the possibility that "God is
self-limited utterly by his creation,...that he bound himself to
time and its hazards and haps as a man would lash himself to
a tree for love." She sees that God as helpless, dependent
upon us, "self-abandoned on the doorstep of time, wondered
at by cattle and oxen." One pauses and considers Bethlehem
again.

 Dillard's question, then, is "whether God touches
anything," or whether there is any "link at the base of
things?" Is there any meaning in our history? In Julie's
history? Or are we and Julie part of "an accidental
universe" which "spins mute, obedient only to its own gross
terms, meaningless, out of mind, and alone."

 In the final chapter Dillard tells us the meaning of her
book's title, *Holy The Firm.* At the base of everything,
beneath all the layers of creation, is a substance which is "in
touch with the Absolute! At base. The name of this
substance is: Holy The Firm." By linking this substance,
this lowliest and dullest of created things, "at base" with the
Absolute, Dillard believes she has brought time and space
together with uncreated reality. Where does this leave Julie
Norwich?

 She sees her as "salted with fire...preserved like a salted
fillet from all evil, baptised at birth into time and now into
eternity, into the blade-like arms of God." She speaks to
her: "You might as well be a nun."

 "Held, held fast by love in the world like the moth in
wax, like a wick, your head on fire with prayer, held utterly,
outside and in, you sleep alone, if you call that alone. You
cry God."

 Then, "Julie Norwich; I know. Surgeons will fix your
face. This will all be a dream, an anecdote, something to tell

your husband one night: I was burned. Or if you're scarred, you're scarred."

These are hard things. There were hard things in Julian's day, the Plague, wars, barbarous punishments, grinding poverty, as there are in our own: apartheid in South Africa, political prisoners in every corner of the world, cancer wards, war-torn women and children in Lebanon or El Salvador or Ireland.

It takes courage to say, as Julian of Norwich did, "All will be well, all manner of thing shall be well." And she who said it first learned it by contemplating suffering, not by hiding from it — the suffering of the Son of God, whom she calls Mother. Annie Dillard in our time shows us that we *can* look at woundedness, much as we prefer to hide from it. It is the first step toward healing.

Vulnerability is being revalued in our contemporary world, not by a theology which sees God as needing victims, or "victim souls," in order to appease anger or draw down mercy — a God, as Frank Gavin once said in a retreat, who can't feel decently toward us until he is placated by buckets of blood, and the blood of his own Son at that. Vulnerability is being revalued because it is a quality of the life of God, and in the obedience of the Son our own acceptance of suffering is made healing.

No one can prove such a claim for accepted suffering. It needs to be set in the perspective of the cross, suffering which was imposed upon Jesus by the sinful powers and historical persons of this world, and in some real way by each of us insofar as we choose sin over faithfulness to the constraints of God's love. God suffers, allows, what we choose. Sometimes our own turn comes to bear unavoidable suffering. It is then that we can turn to God and ask for willingness. This may well be after we have shouted our protests loud and long! But the very asking changes, although it does not abolish, the suffering. It makes it bearable, and, in some obscure way we know by faith and perhaps by experience, it makes us channels of God's healing love. This mystery of accepted suffering is at the heart of the sacraments, of baptism and Eucharist, reconciliation and marriage, as well as the commissioning of ministers and ministries in ordination and confirmation.

What Dillard, Walker, and Nouwen do for us is to hold up some images and tell some stories that point to the beauty and power of the peace-making qualities of life, without denying the violence of nature and society. They show us anew the value of endurance, vulnerability, patience in nurturing, mutuality in love, the disposition to seek for healing rather than conquest, and connectedness rather than the ability to win.

One of the concerns of this book has been to help discover and defend a both/and spirituality, a spirituality for our time which accepts the tension between respect for the earth and the values of human life in the flesh, and the positive wisdom and insight of the great spiritual writings of the Christian tradition. The tension between the two is undeniable, and I do not claim to have relieved it. I believe we live most fully and fruitfully when we live with the tension.

One of the forms this tension takes has been pointed out by Dorothée Soelle in *Death by Bread Alone*, where she raises the question of how to relate "the inward journey which we need for the experience of self" with the return journey into social life and its responsibilities. "Inwardness and involvement are not companion attitudes in most people....Prayer and work, labor and contemplation...appear to be compartmentalized into two worlds, and the experience of groups that try to do both at the same time are too meager and too weak to be discussed." "Meager" and "weak" are hardly adequate to describe the works of social compassion and involvement of many monastic communities, from Basil of Caesarea to Taizé and the Little Brothers and Sisters of Jesus. Nevertheless Soelle puts her finger on a central question, the relationship between interior prayer and the life of action. It is not enough, to say as she does, "living as Christ lived means the inward journey to the emptying and surrender of the ego and the return jouney to the midst of the world." We need to know what resources we have for living as Christ lived in our world.[39]

Living with Apocalypse: Resources for Social Compassion, a collection of essays edited by Tilden Edwards, addresses this need.[40] Rosemary Haughton's chapter, "Liberating the Divine Energy," asks whether we really *can* make society compassionate, and what lies to our hand to help us do it? She recognizes that we need a leap of faith, a longer perspective than our present range, and the courage to act upon such a faith. She calls for a different kind of consciousness, one which deals with Scripture in imaginative ways without disregarding the painstaking work of biblical scholars. Critical judgment is needed, also, in our assessment of the value systems and theological formulations of our traditions, in order to avoid being seduced by cultural assumptions and expectations which tend to obscure or distort the imperatives of Jesus' preaching of the gospel.

She underlines the importance for society as well as for personal wholeness of keeping the intuitive functions working together with the rational. "We need all that patient (and imaginative) scholarship has been able to reveal, because without it imagination has breath but no wings. It has power and elan, but lacks direction and precision, and hence has no cutting edge, no impact on society."

Haughton deals briefly with the problem of patriarchal language in the Bible, which is such an obstacle to prayer and to faith for many women today. Even the words which Jesus uses to point to God's presence among us, "kingdom" or "reign" of heaven, have oppressive connotations. She points out that in the only scriptures Jesus knew, the prophets described the "reign of God" in terms which reflected the political entities of the surrounding nations, but also that they were used to describe not a static hierarchy but a "network of mutually supportive relationships" symbolized, for example, in the unlikely partnership of a lion and a lamb. The God of mercies is the animator and sustainer of a dynamic community which is to reflect in its structures and relationships God's own compassion, as well as God's justice.

The model that she suggests for this kingdom is not a rigid ladder, but a network "in which the strength of the whole net depends on, but cannot control, the integrity of the knots, yet whose greatest area consists of holes!"

The spiritual resources for life in such a kingdom are the same for us as they were for Jesus: allowing ourselves to become involved in the suffering, oppression and limitations of others by listening to those with whom we disagree, becoming aware of the problems of others, of other races and classes and tastes and preferences, and of those of the opposite gender to our own. Such involvement will require us to break through long-sanctified social and religious barriers, and through the forgotten memories of our own painful and humiliating past experiences. The divine energy we see at work in Jesus is the essential reality of our own selves, and the central resource for social compassion.

Suppose we really do this? Suppose we open ourselves to our own woundedness and anger, and also to that of others? How do we survive? How do we become wounded healers rather than Typhoid Marys? Another essay in *Living with Apocalypse*, "Despair and Empowerment Work," by Joanna Rogers Macy, suggests techniques of prayer and self-awareness which may help us confront the darkness of others whom we seek to befriend, without being radically distorted by it.

Many groups in our society are trying to express and protect the values of trust, respect for differences, and compassion through decision-making by consensus, by coming to a common mind, rather than by the direction of someone in charge or by a majority vote. One sees this in groups working for peace and justice, in reflection groups, and more and more, in monastic life where the traditional vow of obedience is lived out in horizontal relationships to everyone in the community, rather than in a vertical relationship to a higher superior. When respect for differences includes respect for expertise and wisdom which may surpass our own, these methods can be very fruitful and energizing; they tend to use rather than to hem in the natural gifts and strengths present in every intentional group. A new consciousness is also arising in our society about the need for justice in the sharing of domestic responsibilities, the importance of sharing with fathers the birth experience and the ongoing nurturing of children.

As the pressure for change, for the reversal of class structures and spiritual values, increases in our society, it is not surprising that a reaction is also setting in strongly in some quarters. Various currents can be detected in the opposition to the change in attitude we have been commending, set in motion by deep-seated fears of the loss of control and privilege, and sanctioned by a literalist interpretation of the sacred writings of various groups, Muslim and Jewish as well as Christian. These militant reactions seem to return us to God, the God of the western world, patriarch, law-giver, warrior and judge.

Still other currents are appearing whose thrust is in the opposite direction, toward a radical reversal of our language about God and a matriarchal divinity — God as mother, healer, peace-maker — which opposes the attribution of fatherhood and sovereignty to God. There are forms of feminism which devalue and deride the male and the masculine, and set up female divinities and powers for us to worship. A new self-image and new attachment is proposed in place of the old.

Is there any other way of responding to the need for a new attitude toward women and the feminine in all of us, men as well as women? Can we learn some detachment from old images without creating new forms of bondage, that is, of attachment?

Gerald May in *Will and Spirit* takes a position which is unusual for a psychotherapist. He accepts the importance of a strong and positive self-image for everyone's maturity and wholeness, but he warns us that we can be excessively attached to our self-image. Such an attachment can lead to self-importance and to that self-centeredness which he calls "willfulness." As we become aware that our attachment to self-image is dragging us down or turning us in upon ourselves, we are faced with the necessity of diminishing that attachment. In short, we are called to "deny ourselves." Such self-denial is a taking up of our cross, a painful and frightening thing to do. It can be dangerous. We can get lost. Hence he writes, "The process of relinquishing attachment must be surrounded with guidance, discernment, tradition, community, scripture, critique and prayer....The contemplative response is so radical, so apparently presumptuous, that it stretches us to the very limits of our rationality. The contemplative answer is this: 'As attachment ceases to be a motivation, our actions become experiences of divine love.'"[41] I have tried to talk about Scripture and tradition in such a way as to help us begin the dangerous journey from attachment to patterns of self-understanding and relationship toward more fluid categories of mutuality, without jettisoning observance, discipline, Scripture and tradition.

The theological underpinning for such a socially-oriented spirituality is found in the doctrine of the Holy Trinity, which is both the pattern of the life of God and the pattern of God's relationship with us, and hence the pattern of all social life. We now turn to look at some contemporary approaches to this central article of faith. We shall see that there are intimations of the new directions trinitarian doctrine seems to be taking.

This book is trying to maintain an alternative to a contemporary spirituality which has become vague and sentimental by losing touch with the intellectual clarity and moral certainties of earlier theological systems. I have not found fundamentalist neo-patriarchy, on the one hand, nor an exclusive matriarchy, on the other, to be acceptable solutions. Without denying that God is mother, healer, and peacemaker, I do assert that God is also law-giver, teacher, guide, and judge. Yet I insist further that all these metaphors pointing toward God must be interpreted by the supreme quality of love, the compassionate womb-love of God that overarches and interprets all the other attributes.

Since we are made in the image of the triune God, we need a trinitarian theology which provides us with a stable point of reference. Such a theology, stated in terms of love, implies mutuality, wholeness, creativity and the equality of all persons.

The doctrine of the Holy Trinity arose from experience, not from theory. The experience was that of the first Christian community as its members began to appropriate the gifts of Pentecost in their communal life, the new creation in the Holy Spirit. As succeeding generations recorded their reflections on this experience, they began to elucidate and preserve its meaning in liturgy, devotional writings, intellectual speculation and conciliar decrees. The earliest credal statements expressed doctrine in philosophical terms borrowed from contemporary Hellenism; they are terms which are very difficult to translate into everyday English speech, because they cannot be understood concretely except in relationship to the Platonic system from which they derive. The creeds also reflect the strongly patriarchal culture of their origin, with a hierarchy of values which sets power, rather than the relationship of love, at the top of the scale. Joseph Bracken offers an alternative approach to the doctrine of the Trinity when he suggests that we begin by "thinking of God as a process of self-giving love rather than as the Pure Act of Being."[42]

We have seen that Augustine started something new when he identified the image of God in us with the Holy Trinity. In his treatise on the Trinity Augustine has several ways of imaging it. One is intra-personal: he entered within himself and discovered in the triad of memory, reason, and will a reflection of the triune Godhead. Another is interpersonal, based on the relationship between the persons of the Trinity as lover, beloved, and love. Augustine does not develop the social implications of either of these images of the Trinity, but in the twelfth century Richard of St. Victor found and elaborated on the second, interpersonal theme. Julian of Norwich is restating Augustine when she says that "the blessed Trinity made mankind in their image and likeness," and places all in one perspective when she claims, "Love is our Lord's meaning." "For of all the attributes of the Blessed Trinity, it is God's will that we have most confidence in his delight and his love."[43]

Medieval theologians had argued from Augustine's triad of lover, beloved, and love that because God is love there must be self-giving and receiving of love between the persons of the Godhead. In the eighteenth century the philosophers of the Enlightenment also looked within, but saw not the trinities of Augustine, but one sovereign God. The God of the philosophers was personal, that is, in a new sense of being a center of consciousness — rational, absolute, the lord of creation. In consequence, these philosophers tended to see human beings as little lords of creation, rational and personal individuals. Communities were simply groups of these individuals.

Although this rationalist view of God as unified personal subject inherited from the eighteenth century has never officially modified creeds or decrees of councils, it has certainly modified and confused our thinking about God as Holy Trinity and about ourselves as creatures made in God's image. Individual and personal ideas and values that are necessary both for creativity and for moral and spiritual development were not sufficiently related to the sub-human orders of creation, nor to the structures of society.

We turn to feminist theology and to liberation theology in search of a doctrine of the Trinity which begins with self-giving love. Few feminist theologians today have any use for the Trinity because they regard it as hopelessly enmeshed with a Father/Son relationship, an exclusively male image of God. There are exceptions, however, among them Patricia Wilson-Kastner: "The notion of the Trinity is based on the self-revelation of a God who is at heart relational, not a bare unity or an isolated divine monarch."[44] Liberation theology, which approaches these questions from another angle, does not arise from classical or scholastic disputations, nor from the philosophical speculations of a bourgeois intelligentsia. It arises rather from a dialogue between three groups in the Third World: the poor and oppressed workers, peasants, and indigenous groups; social activists and populist leaders; and theologians and scholars from university circles. This dialogue focuses not just upon theology but also upon "praxis," the actual expression in concrete contemporary history of the inbreaking of the kingdom announced by the Jesus of history, and the reflection upon that inbreaking. Beginning as he does with a faith commitment to Jesus, Gustavo Gutierrez, one of the leading liberation theologians of Latin America, comes to the conclusion that "the basis for brotherhood (and sisterhood) is full communion with the Persons of the Holy Trinity."[45]

A theology of the Trinity which begins with three divine persons in relationship, instead of with an abstract unity, moves toward an understanding of the divine nature as suffering and as servant rather than as invulnerable sovereign. In the light of their own experience of suffering and of servanthood, of being in the lowest place, disposed of by others, simple people, such as indigenous Indian peasants of South and Central America and urban workers in Europe, have begun to come together in "base communities" to reflect upon Scripture. They seek from it a source of guidance for understanding their oppression, and for the hope, energy and vision to accomplish the work of social transformation. Grounded in Scripture, especially as it is understood by the poor and dispossessed of our western world, liberation theology points toward a God whose supreme attribute is neither power nor reason, but suffering love. This theology faces into the mystery of the death of God, the abandonment of the Son by the Father, and the grief and suffering of the Father in the death of the Son.

This aspect of liberation theology poses problems for us. Recently I came upon a statement in my parish bulletin which startled me. The writer was explaining his design for new vestments, and wrote, "The two contrasting color blocks remind us of Jesus' divine and human natures which were beaten and humiliated." My first reaction was to recoil from such language. How can you "beat up" a nature? The divine nature cannot be beaten up or humiliated. However, as I thought about it more carefully, I realized that I was "doing theology from above," beginning with rational statements about God rather than beginning "from below" with experience, with Jesus' life and death. Without stumbling over the proprieties of speech, is there not a way in which God can be beaten and humiliated? And is not the passion of Jesus at the pillar and on the cross just that?

The theologian Jurgen Moltmann sums up the theological justification for such a position: "What happens in Jesus' passion is the giving up of the Son through the Father. In giving up his own Son, God cuts himself off from himself and sacrifices his own self. The giving up of the Son reveals a pain in God which can only be understood in Trinitarian terms, or not at all." Reginald Fuller comments on this theology that if we start from the experience and suffering of Jesus, then we can begin to "speak, cautiously, of a crucified God or of the death of God....as a profound expression of the depth of God's involvement in the cross."[46]

In all of this we can make out signs of a basic theological shift. These theologians are turning from concepts of the Trinity and of the divine unity based on dominance and power to wrestling with ideas of a "crucified God," powerless in all senses but one — the freedom to love. The importance of new and emerging interpretations of the Trinity for the self-understanding of women is clear. Women as well as men can find their own patterns in the relational life of the Godhead, as they cannot so easily do when the distinction between the three divine persons is based upon the notion of "origin." "Father, Son and Holy Spirit" is not the only way of describing the Persons; "life-giver, pain-bearer, and love-maker" is an alternative with which people of both genders can identify.

In the image of God, male and female, God created us all. This creator God who is revealed in Scripture is mother and father, seed and womb, mercy and power, one God. God's image in us reflects freedom, sovereignty and compassionate love in harmonious union. We see this image supremely in Christ and, less clearly, in every man and woman. There is a loving going out in self-giving at the center of God's life which reveals to us the lover, the beloved, and love in the inner life of God. God is triune, we say. The Holy Trinity is our pattern.

One way in which each individual reflects the triune God is by the acceptance of the polarity within each of us. Masculine and feminine qualities in infinitely varying proportions and interactions live in our deepest selves. Our life task, from this perspective, is integration: freeing, developing, enjoying, using our opposite qualities in creative tension. It is in meeting that new life is born, new ideas are generated; works of art, visions and workable plans for peace and justice emerge. In order to receive the other, the opposite, we must surrender our boundaries, our safe perimeters, moats and fortresses, and be undefended. We die to our isolation, our self-image as we ourselves construct, define and defend it, when we enter into truly reciprocal relationships of respect and love. This is the primary task of marriage, of friendship and of community. Offspring, works of beauty and usefulness and delight, mission and vision, are the fruits of this meeting with the opposite.

We are called to this fruitfulness at every level of our experience: within ourselves, in prayer and contemplation, repentance and self-offering, in relationships of friendship and marriage; in small groups for work or reflection or celebration; and in the great collectives of our culture. Yes, even there! In the structures of church and state, industry and technology, the image of the Kingdom can be manifested. Liturgical prayer, especially the prayers of the Eucharist, can be an effective force for forming our collectives so that they reflect justice and peace, the *shalom* of God.

Since being made in the image of God includes sharing in the divine sovereignty, we are free, really free, to make choices. The help we need to make good choices, which theologians call grace, is by its nature a gift and not an imposition. We can and often do refuse it, and obscure the divine image in ourselves.

Theologians also tell us that the image of God in us is indelible and unblemishable. It can never be wholly obliterated. The word "image" in our culture, however, is commonly used in a different sense. It carries a connotation of falsity. Manufacturers are concerned with the "image" of their product and their corporate entity, and seek to project a "positive image" through advertising. "Project" is a tell-tale word, for it implies that the qualities of beauty and comfort and helpfulness attributed to a product are not intrinsic to it, but are supplied from outside. When we fail to receive the glamor, safety, pleasure and economies we are promised, we are aware that the image is false. Like gravity, like the imprint on a seed, the indelible divine image is intrinsic. It can be hidden, denied, or obscured, but it cannot be erased or deformed in itself.

In behavioral psychology "self-image" is sometimes presented as a goal in itself. We are impressed with the importance of developing a strong self-image. This is not a fantasy, like so much of advertising, because it is true — we do need a healthy self-image. When, however, our self-image becomes the object of our concern and protection and even worship, instead of a symbol pointing beyond itself to our true meaning and origin, it leads to idolatry. The image becomes an idol.

Another kind of distortion occurs when we accept the duality of our human nature with its gender polarity, but deny the equal worth and beauty and importance of the two poles, male and female, feminine and masculine, and exalt one over the other. For millennia we have been immersed in a culture which does just this — exalts the male over the female, romanticizes the masculine, and trivializes the feminine. We are urgently required to recognize the danger of these distortions and work hard to readjust the balance. We need to raise up into memory and esteem qualities and persons long been forgotten or assigned to inferiority and even to oppression. The call to us as feminine and masculine, as both/and, is a call to reflect our creator as the pattern of every human individual and every human community by accepting and rejoicing in the authentic qualities that go with each pole of the human continuum. Our obedience to this vocation will empower us to accept with joy and respect, giving and taking, gifts from each other in the God-given freedom of our nature, the freedom to love.

There are not many representations of the Holy Trinity in art, and the ones we have are often unsuccessful. Two men and a dove somehow fail to help me understand the mystery of God in whose image I am made. But the Russian icon painters, especially Andrei Rublev, have used a different approach which draws us to enter the mystery reverently and gratefully. Rublev has taken the story from the 18th chapter of Genesis of the visit to Abraham of three strangers, and used it as an icon, a place to meet God. The three strangers, poor men needing food and a bed, are also angels representing the three divine persons. As strangers they carry staves, and as angels, neither man nor woman, they are winged. They are seated at the table of hospitality which

Abraham and Sarah have provided in accordance with the law of hospitality. The angels incline slightly toward each other, in a relationship which is profound and mutual. The circular composition of the figures links them in a common expression of sadness and resolution as they regard the lamb at the center of the table, and the cup, symbol of the coming sacrifice. As in the story of Genesis, the three are also one, and they are God.

This icon has been called the archetypal prayer, and women as well as men may without distortion be drawn up into it and find a meeting place with God. Love is our Lord's meaning, and love is the meaning of the Trinity, and it is our meaning.

NOTES

[1]Cited in Phyllis Trible, *God and the Rhetoric of Sexuality* (Philadelphia, 1978), p. 16. This whole chapter owes much to her close analysis of texts and sensitivity to poetic form.

[2]Gerhard von Rad, *Genesis* (Philadelphia, 1982), p. 26.

[3]Ibid, p. 81.

[4]See ps. 103:8,13; Dt. 13:18; Lev. 3:32; 1 Sam. 2:7,8.

[5]Elizabeth Schuessler Fiorenza, *In Memory of Her* (New York, 1984), pp. 47, 178.

[6]"Gnosticism" covers a wide variety of ideas and beliefs, and its adherents had a tendency to merge with and influence orthodox religions in the second century C.E. Gnostics taught a dualistic view of the universe and of the human being, in which material things are evil, and salvation is to be obtained through secret knowledge, or *gnosis*.

[7]Rosemary Ruether, *Sexism and God Talk* (Boston, 1983), pp. 60ff.

[8]Ibid, pp. 135, 137, 138.

[9]Patricia Wilson-Kastner, *Faith, Feminism, and the Christ* (Philadelphia, 1983), p. 90.

[10]*On Virginity*, Nicene and Post-Nicene Fathers (Grand Rapids, MI, 1972) 5:345, 347, 352.

[11]*On the Soul and the Resurrection*, Nicene and Post-Nicene Fathers (Grand Rapids, MI, 1972) 5:467.

[12]*The Life of Moses*, 3. 163.

[13]*La Vie de Macrine, Sources Chretiennes* 178 (Paris, 1971), sec's 10, 11, 18, 22.

[14]*The Greater Catechism*, Nicene and Post-Nicene Fathers (Grand Rapids, MI, 1972) 5:505-6.

[15]*Confessions*, 9. 24.

[16]Cited in L. Bouyer, *The Spirituality of the New Testament and the Fathers* (London, 1963), p. 479.

[17]*On the Christian Combat*, 31. 33.

[18]*On the Nature of the Good*, 48.

[19]*The City of God*, 15. 7.

[20]*On the Trinity*, 12. 6. 6, 7.

[21]G. L. Prestige, *God in Patristic Thought* (London, 1952), p. 236.

[22]*Soliloquies* 1, 13, 22.

[23]Thomas Merton, *Raids on the Unspeakable* (New York, 1964), p. 160.

[24]*La Vita Nuova*, trans. B. Reynolds (New York, 1964), p. 29.

[25]From Dorothy Sayers' introduction to her translation of the *Inferno*, p. xxvi. The quotations from *The Divine Comedy* in this chapter follow the Penguin edition of Sayers' translation in three volumes (New York, 1950, 1955, 1962).

[26]William Anderson, *Dante the Maker* (New York, 1982), p. 88.

[27]Ibid, p. 110.

[28]Charles Williams, *The Figure of Beatrice* (London, 1943), pp. 58, 72.

[29]Daniel Berrigan, *The Discipline of the Mountain* (New York, 1979), p. 21.

[30]Julian of Norwich, *Showings*, Edmund Colledge and James Walsh, eds. (New York, 1978), pp. 125, 127.

[31]Thomas Merton, *Conjectures of a Guilty Bystander* (Garden City, NY, 1968), p. 212.

[32]Julian of Norwich, *Revelations of Divine Love*, M. L. del Mastro, ed. (Garden City, NY, 1977), p. 69.

[33]*The Nun's Rule, Being the Ancrene Riwle Modernized*, James Morton, ed. (New York, 1966), pp. 52, 55.

[34]Introduction to *Showings*, p. 3.

[35]Merton, p. 211.

[36]Alice Walker, *The Color Purple* (New York, 1982), pp. 1, 177-8, 229-30, 238, 249.

[37]Henri Nouwen, *The Wounded Healer* (New York, 1972), p. iv.

[38]Annie Dillard, *Holy the Firm* (Toronto, 1979), pp. 31, 82, 134.

[39]Dorothee Soelle, *Death by Bread Alone* (Philadelphia, 1978), pp. 56, 135.

[40]Tilden Edwards, ed. *Living with Apocalypse: Spiritual Resources for Social Compassion* (San Francisco, 1984), pp. 76, 82, 182, 86.

[41]Gerald May, *Will and Spirit* (San Francisco, 1982), p. 258.

[42]Joseph A. Bracken, SJ, *What Are They Saying About the Trinity?* (New York, 1979), p. 60.

[43]*Showings*, pp. 195, 342, 168.

[44]*Faith, Feminism, and the Christ*, p. 124.

[45]Gustavo Gutierrez, *A Theology of Liberation* (New York, 1973), p. 265.

[46]Jurgen Moltmann, *The Trinity and the Kingdom* (San Francisco, 1981), p. 83; Reginald Fuller and Pheme Perkins, *Who Is the Christ?* (Philadelphia, 1983), p. 118.